A COURSE IN SPIRIT

A COURSE IN SPIRITUAL PHILOSOPHY

Madam Amanda Valiant

Edited by Alan Valiant

MERLIN BOOKS LTD.
Braunton Devon.

©Madam Amanda Valiant, 1991
First published in Great Britain, 1991

British Library Cataloguing in Publication Data
Valiant, Amanda 1925-1988
A course of spiritual philosophy.
1. Spiritualism
I. Title
133.901
ISBN 0-86303-550-7

ISBN 0 86303 550-7
Printed in England by Antony Rowe Ltd., Chippenham, Wilts.

A COURSE IN SPIRITUAL PHILOSOPHY
by
MADAM AMANDA VALIANT

Unique in history, the Course has been compiled from information passed to Madam Amanda Valiant by the highest beings in the spiritual universe during hundreds of communications. Owing to the use of a highly-developed and instantaneous method of conversing with those in the spiritual world, Amanda has been in daily touch with those whose knowledge and wisdom are supreme.

Reincarnated in order to try to arouse public interest in the spiritual existence, Amanda is helping many people by explaining the facts about their being, the reasons for their suffering and what they must do to rise spiritually.

Most of the knowledge taught is unique and is unknown to anyone who has not already taken the course. Numerous, contemporary enigmas are explained as are many of the mysteries of biblical events. The Course teaches that, when knowledge is available, belief is unnecessary.

There is no religious belief expressed because wisdom is superior and Amanda Valiant is an independent psychic researcher, unaffiliated to any other organization. To those already on the 'path', the Amanda Valiant Course in Spiritual Philosophy will save them years of fruitless searching, since many of the facts revealed are available from no other source.

In addition to acquiring knowledge hitherto kept secret by the Spiritual Hierarchy, the Course student will find his or her life change for the better as understanding replaces doubt, as knowledge is substituted for belief and as revelation opens up the psychic awareness of the student. One's ability is increased to the extent that one KNOWS!

The student's value as a spiritual human being is enhanced to the degree that he or she comprehends the reasons for the unpleasant and the pleasant things that happen to him or her. The Course shows the student that life is anything but random, that there is a purpose, that man is not the result of a biological accident and that man is immortal. This implies that one's behaviour while incarnate is of the utmost significance.

Spiritual progression has to be worked at continuously if one is to break the reincarnation cycle but few people know how best to progress. Many rely upon religious teachings to carry them through life. Some succeed in rising but many do not because mere belief in a dogma cannot guarantee deliverance to the higher realms in heaven.

In Part II of the Course, the names of the Spiritual Hierarchy are revealed and the student is shown a chart showing the Planes in Heaven and their significance. Many of the puzzling aspects of biblical events are explained, such as what *really* happened to Jesus Christ, and His true purpose on earth.

This remarkable book contains scripts written by God and Jesus Christ through the hand of Amanda Valiant. This is the first time in history that such direct communication has been received from the Spiritual Hierarchy!

CONTENTS

Introduction ... 9

Part One
Lesson 1: 'In the Beginning....' ... 11
Lesson 2: The Chart of Spiritual Existence ... 21
Lesson 3: The Akashic Record ... 34
Lesson 4: Reincarnation and Kharma ... 43
Lesson 5: Responsibility and Right Thinking ... 59
Lesson 6: The Mind ... 68
Lesson 7: Communication Comprehension ... 78
Lesson 8: The Harmony and Discord Scale ... 86
Lesson 9: The Kingdom of Heaven ... 91

Part Two
Lesson 10: Jesus Christ — the Truth ... 97
Lesson 11: God's Role in the Universe ... 110
Lesson 12: Sphere Eight and the Lord God ... 122
Lesson 13: The Inhabited Planets ... 131
Lesson 14: Moses and the Commandments ... 139
Lesson 15: Why Religions, and Individual Personality ... 150
Lesson 16: The New Beginning ... 157

Conclusion ... 161
Sonnet by William Shakespeare ... 163

INTRODUCTION

In Redruth, in Cornwall, on 20th July, 1925, a child was born whose true purpose and destiny were not to become apparent until she had lived for fifty years.

Destined to suffer at the hands of ignorant, suppressive people, Amanda fought with all her might against the treatment meted out to her, not only by her employers and her own family, those whom she held most dear, but even by staff while she was in the maternity hospital.

Her mother passed on when Amanda was only nine years old. This had a profound adverse effect upon her and the psychosomatic result of this was to leave her with rheumatic fever and a complete block on her memory before that time.

Amanda married as soon as possible in order to escape further suppression but, after bringing up three children and being treated as a slave all her married life, she had had enough and was forced to divorce her husband. A few years later, she and I were brought together by an amazing sequence of events, neither of us knowing at the time what remarkable experiences we were to share in the future.

We discovered that we were both interested in the spiritual existence and then I was prompted to attempt to communicate with the spiritual world. Using my knowledge of research and development acquired during my professional career, I perfected a method, after which Amanda and I began to receive astounding information, at first from our deceased relatives and, later, from members of the Spiritual Hierarchy.

Amanda was told that she had been incarnated for a special purpose after having been trained under the supervision of the Lord God. Unfortunately, owing to the manner in which she was treated, her planned kharma did not work out in the way that it was intended.

The highest standards of ethics were practised by Amanda, higher than those of anyone whom I have ever known. She would never close the door to anyone in need of help, even though they had treated her badly.

Through constant suffering including angina, arthritis, diabetes and severe loss of hearing, Amanda battled on doing more work in a week than the average hard-working person. After doing the chores in our home, she would sit at her typewriter for hours, writing materials for the college that she founded, 'The College of Alithology (The Study of Truth)', in which she was successful in improving the lives of many students who would, otherwise, have had serious difficulties.

Not only did Amanda type numerous scripts for both her own and my work but she wrote many letters in reply to the questions posed by the students of her correspondence course which forms the main part of this work.

Amanda's indomitable spirit, in spite of her many physical problems, was an example to all who knew her and she re-shaped the lives of many people who were struggling with the vicissitudes of existence. Those who had physical complaints received healing from her and those with emotional problems received counselling of a unique kind, combined as it was with her ability to consult a person's Akashic Record, thereby enabling her to discover the origin of the problem.

From 1975 until her passing from a heart attack on 4th November, 1988, Amanda and I were in daily communication with numerous spiritual beings and, in particular, members of the Spiritual Hierarchy, a privilege that I still enjoy in order to enable me to carry on trying to spread the truth as it has been given to us by the Hierarchy.

Amanda passed while half-way through her postal course in spiritual philosophy. I, then, completed the course under her supervision from her new position in Sphere Eight in Heaven.

It is hoped that the information contained in this book will reach a much wider readership and fill the enormous gap between 'belief' and 'knowledge'.

Because we worked together, Amanda and I were able to check each other's communication and this is why I am able to endorse and confirm all of the information contained in the following pages. Those genuine seekers of the truth need look no further. It is presented *here*!

Alan Valiant

Lesson 1   Part One

'IN THE BEGINNING. . . .'

Philosophers and seekers of the truth of their existence have produced numerous theories and a few have had the insight and discernment to arrive at evidence of the spiritual existence that is confirmatory. It is, though, the person who establishes direct links with those in Heaven, who is in the best possible position to elicit the facts concerning that region and that phase in our being.

Having had a very strong interest in everything connected with spiritual subjects since the tender age of fifteen years, and I am now of retirement age, I, too, have acquired knowledge as a result of my studies and persistent seeking.

While we are not permitted to know *everything* about the next world, we *are* allowed to know a very great deal, which is contrary to the opinions expressed by less well-informed people. This knowledge is available to all those who *really* want to know it through this Course. In all the lessons I shall explain things which may have puzzled you for decades.

Apart from time and a quiet place for studying, another essential requirement is self-discipline. Spiritual facts cannot be assimilated in a few hours and sincere dedication to this subject, which is deep but fascinating, is vital to your spiritual evolution.

During hundreds of hours of communication with people in the 'other world', I have spoken with those who were happy, sad, serious, learned, ignorant, hilariously funny, timid, bold, weak, strong, and with those who were arrogant. I established a wonderful rapport with all kinds of people, from High Spiritual Beings in the upper realms of Heaven, to those on the lower Planes. These lessons are the result of my experience.

Most people are under the misapprehension that the moment one sets foot in the spiritual world, a magic wand is waved and everything is immediately perfect. Unfortunately, this is not the case for, 'As a man thinks, so is he.' You are probably very familiar with that quotation. How true it is! Those whose minds are rich in goodness, beauty, kindness and truth accept their new surroundings in Heaven after their passing, more readily than those who thought only negatively throughout their lives.

1. The Reasons for Incarnating

We are born into this world for a definite reason. Some come to teach others and Jesus Christ is a well-known example of this. Quite a few arrive on Earth because they have lessons to learn such as the cultivation of patience, unselfishness or humility. However, most of us are here to atone for past indiscretions, in addition to the improvement of personality traits.

We do not arrive on Earth completely innocent or ignorant. We bring with us a large store of knowledge that is contained in our subconscious minds and which has been gathered during many lifetimes. In some people this subliminal awareness can be heavily laden with guilt associated with wicked deeds that they committed in their previous lives. This subject will be enlarged upon in a later lesson.

2. The Heavenly Environment

Pictorially and geographically, Earth is a reflection of Heaven. There are many places of great beauty on Earth which attract tourists who stand, admire and wonder. Heaven has its scenery too, such as buildings of magnificent design, rivers, forests, seas, houses, gardens, parks, fountains, flowers, birds, and animals. The colours cannot be described, for they are so beautiful and Earth has nothing with which they can be compared.

Spiritual beings can dress or remain naked as they wish. Nudity is ignored in Heaven. It is not treated as a subject for ridicule and bawdy remarks as it is on Earth. Extremes of heat or cold are not felt because the atmosphere is comfortable to spiritual beings. People usually dress in the manner and custom of their period when they were incarnate. Some of the costumes worn are very colourful indeed, especially the Elizabethan ones.

Overall, there is an atmosphere of peace, tolerance, love, understanding and tranquillity among the inhabitants of Heaven that is difficult for us mere mortals to grasp.

3. *How they Communicate*

Communication between spiritual beings is achieved either by word of mouth or by thought transference, otherwise known as telepathy. One little girl in the spiritual world summed it up admirably when she was being interviewed by psychic researchers. She was asked how speech was relayed in Heaven and her answer was, "We talk with our think!"

4. *How they Move and Travel*

If they wish, spiritual beings can walk from place to place, just as we do, but they seem to prefer gliding or floating. Owing to the fact that there is no space in the sense in which we know it on Earth, it is possible for a spiritual being to be anywhere by merely thinking. For example, if a spiritual being wishes to travel to Earth to be with loved ones left behind, he or she has only to *think* of being at the place where they are and he or she is instantly there. This demonstrates that the power of thought when discarnate should not be underestimated.

5. *The Heavenly 'Time'*

There is no time in Heaven as we know it on Earth. One of the outstanding features noticed by new arrivals in the other world is the, apparently, timeless existence in which they seem to be. This was very obvious during my many conversations with spiritual beings. I was frequently asked by them, "How long have I been here in Heaven?"

Their 'time' is an illusion created by a series of events. When one event has come to pass, so much 'time' has elapsed. Since a spiritual being is immortal, time is irrelevant.

6. *The Emotions of Spiritual Beings*

Spiritual beings are not much different from incarnate people except that they feel no pain. A jolly-natured person is still jolly, whereas a solemn-natured person retains that characteristic. They may eat, drink, taste, feel, see, hear, and smell. The lower entities feel and express hatred, revenge, jealousy and spite.

Relationships that were rather strained when the people concerned were incarnate do not have to be continued upon arrival in Heaven and the persons affected need not meet each other if they do not wish to do so.

Spiritual beings experience a depth of emotional feeling which is much more acute than any felt while incarnate. Remorse at their behaviour, especially if a loved one or close one were involved, can be worse than the greatest grief expressed on Earth.

Some spiritual beings cannot rid themselves of remorse and cling to the scene of their guilt. Others cannot leave the place where they experienced a harrowing trauma of some kind. Conversely, some are loath to leave a scene where they were intensely happy. This could be the reason for reported hauntings of houses and other places.

Those who are capable of love find that their love is unencumbered by physiological or sociological considerations. The ability to recognize one's failings and errors is easier when discarnate because of the acquisition of deeper understanding. This is made possible by the spiritual being's own viewing of situations from a detached position.

7. *Pets and Plants in Heaven*

All animals have a spiritual counterpart which, after having completed its time on Earth, returns to Heaven. Again, contrary to opinions expressed by less well-informed people, animals *do* have souls. They have thoughts and feelings too. Anyone who has a favourite pet can have it with them in Heaven. In fact, every living thing has a spiritual counterpart that returns to Heaven upon death. Even plants and flowers are sentient and it has often been reported that people talk to their plants which produced a definite response.

Plants and flowers are in a special category. They are endowed with a life-force that is not individuated and therefore they are not spiritual beings. As with animals and humans, plants die the moment the life-force, which is a spiritual energy, leaves them and that occurs, either when their life span has been run or they are injured.

Plants and flowers respond to human emotion and this has been proved scientifically in controlled experiments which showed that plants thrived when loved and withered when abused.

8. *The Nature of Death*

When we pass to the other world, we are still *very* real people. It is surprising how many incarnate persons think of a spiritual being as 'a wisp of thin air'. Death is a rebirth. We have a spiritual body that lives inside our physical body for our allotted time on Earth. At death, the spiritual body leaves the physical one usually helped by those in the spiritual world who have been trained in such matters. The silver cord that joins the spiritual body to the physical one parts, and life in a new dimension begins.

Our spiritual body feels as solid to us when we are in the other world as our physical body felt to us when we were in this world. We retain our characteristics and our personalities whether they were good or bad.

The spiritual body does not contain any organs, for example, a heart, a liver, lungs or kidneys because these are unnecessary for survival in the spiritual world.

Some people believe that after they die they become instantly wise and knowledgeable. This is not so. We are the same immediately *after* death as we were *before,* with the same knowledge and the same acquired skills. We take nothing with us but these and our attitudes.

9. *The description of an actual passing*

I should like to conclude this first lesson with an account of the last hours on Earth, and the equivalent of the first few hours in Heaven, of a lady who was known to me. This lady, whom I shall call Joan, died recently and I consider that her story of what happened to her and how she felt at the time, will greatly interest and comfort thousands of incarnate people who fear so-called death.

"My name is Joan and I died of malignant tumours of the brain and lung and suffered terrible pain and agony for many months previously. During the latter part of my illness, I was constantly in and out of my physical body. While I was in it, I thought that it was strange to see my mother, father and other members of my family and friends who, I knew, had died.

"I remember seeing myself lying in the hospital bed with members of the medical profession gathered around me trying to sort me out. Finally, the hospital staff gave my family permission to take me home with them.

"On my final day on Earth, I was out of my earthly body for most of the time. I remember standing in the bedroom I was occupying in my son's house, when I felt a hand touch my shoulder. I turned to see a very lovely lady dressed in blue and she said to me, 'We must go now.' I did not feel frightened or disturbed in any way by her presence.

"For a while I stood there, then I heard my son, Peter, coming up to my room to see how I was getting on but he found that I was no longer occupying my earthly body. He looked very taken aback. I approached him and placed my arms around his shoulders to try to comfort him. I knew that he felt my presence because he looked first at my body on the bed, then around the room.

"He closed my eyes, kissed me and placed the sheet over my body. His next action was to hurry out of the room. I followed him out of the door or, actually, *through* the door. I was amazed! He went to the bathroom and I followed him. He washed his face and then looked into the bedroom again to see, well, I don't know, I don't think he believed that I was dead.

"I followed him downstairs but, instead of walking down the stairs, I seemed to glide, not *on* them but just *above* them. It was, at the time, a strange sensation but I have got used to it now. My friend in blue was standing at the bottom of the stairs. I had completely forgotten about her. She spoke so gently as she offered me her hand and said again, 'We must go now.'

"I was very confused because I did not want to leave Peter. I did not know if I was coming back, or when, and I thought that he might miss me if I was gone for too long. My lady friend encouraged me and told me not to worry as my family would be all right. I thought it strange that she seemed to know what I was thinking because I had not spoken a word. I held her hand and, together, we went.

"I noticed that I no longer had any pain and had a marvellous feeling that I was free. After so many months of pain and anxiety, imagine my surprise and joy at their absence. I then realized that I was naked so I covered myself up. My friend came to the rescue again. She read my thoughts and explained to me that I no longer had the need to wear clothes but that I could if I so desired. She said that she would dress me in a white robe to cover my spiritual body.

"My lady friend, whose name is Samantha, took me to a house. I did not know where it was, but I felt very at ease with this lady and she helped me a great deal. We entered the house and she took me into a sitting-room. It was very nice and the décor would have been my choice.

"She enquired if I would like a cup of tea. I replied that I would. She left the room and came back a few *moments* later with a tray of tea and biscuits. Please notice that I stress *moments* and not *minutes*; this is because it did seem like only seconds before she re-entered the room.

"I sat with my tea and my thoughts. Samantha spoke to me. I saw that her lips were not moving and sounds were not coming from her mouth but still I could hear her speak. Picking up my thoughts, she explained that we *can* speak by telepathy or by word of mouth if we wish. I found this most intriguing and interesting and she went on to explain that we communicate by thought and that all actions are achieved by thought processes.

"Then I remembered my son. I apologized to Samantha and told her that I must leave and go back; then I thought, 'Go back to where? If I had left Earth, where was I now?' I panicked. Samantha gently explained that I was in Heaven and no longer existed in a physical body on Earth. It was then that the full impact that I was dead hit me. I felt overcome with emotion and just sat there and cried. My friend came over to me, put her arms around me and sent loving thoughts to me.

"At this point I heard a knock at the door. I smartened myself up and my friend went to answer the door. I thought I heard voices. Voices? Then I remembered Samantha's words about thought processes. I knew the voices! I remembered and recognized them! To my delighted astonishment, I saw my mother, father and others of my family coming towards me. I was choked with emotion. Everyone seemed so well and young, it was FANTASTIC!

"We all sat in the sitting-room of this lovely little house, which Samantha told me was mine, drinking tea and eating biscuits. It was like a reunion of family and old friends, except that they were all spiritual beings long rid of their earthly bodies.

"Seeing everyone so happy and relaxed made me feel very much at ease. I could not get over my amazement that they were all so young-looking and free from the crippling infirmities that I knew they suffered from when on Earth. After what seemed like no time at all, my family and friends left, leaving Samantha and me alone. I was not afraid to see them go because I knew they would come back to see me again. As I stood at the door waving goodbye, I saw the beautiful trees and flowers that lined the paths leading from my home. It was a marvellous sight, one that everyone dreams of while on Earth, a lovely home in the countryside with beautiful flowers adorning the front garden and here it was, all mine!

"Samantha and I went back into the house and sat down. I then wondered if it was summer here as the only way that I could describe the climate was, 'very comfortable'. Samantha told me that the climate here was never cold but remained comfortable all the time. This was very good news to me because when I was in my earthly body I felt the cold keenly.

"We then went for a walk to explore my new surroundings. We went into the garden at the back of the house, it was filled with lovely flowers and some green trees. Although there were trees, they did not seem to darken the house which was all very bright. I noticed, during our tour, that there were people in different costumes. Some were dressed in period costumes and some in the modern-day style. In some parts, the houses were detached and in other parts there were streets of houses. I saw lakes, countryside landscape, more trees and flowers and everything was so beautiful with breathtakingly wonderful colours.

"We did not seem to be gone from my house very long yet it must have been hours. We had achieved so much. Samantha explained that, here, time did not matter; it had no significance.

"We returned to my house and it looked prettier than before. My friend asked me what I thought of my new home and its surroundings and I could not find words adequate to answer. All I could think of was, 'It's beautiful.'

"I remember thinking that if this is what it is like to be dead, well, I quite like the idea. While I was in my earthly body, I was afraid of dying because my religion could not offer any solution as to what lay beyond death. Through my own experience of death and discovering what happens afterwards, I can truthfully say that dying is nothing to be afraid of. With the knowledge that I have gained since returning to Heaven, I would far rather be here in my spiritual body than struggling on Earth in a physical one."

Summary of Lesson 1 Part One

From this lesson we have learned the following facts:
1. We do not die, we are born again.
2. We enter another world which is almost as familiar to us as the physical world that we have just left.
3. We have a spiritual body similar in appearance to the physical body that we had on Earth.
4. We are the same person the moment after death as we were the moment before death.
5. We no longer feel pain and physical problems no longer exist.
6. The spiritual body does not contain any organs such as a heart, a liver, lungs or kidneys, to trouble us as they may have done while we were incarnate.
7. We are given opportunities to learn anything we wish and to progress spiritually.

Lesson 2   **Part One**

THE CHART OF SPIRITUAL EXISTENCE

Heaven consists of several Planes or Levels of Existence but I shall refer to them as Planes. All of these will be explained and dealt with during the Course but, for this lesson, I shall only talk about Planes One to Five. As you read the description of each Plane, please study the chart given with this lesson.

There is no fiery, burning hell as preached in some religions. The planet Earth is the *only* hell and people make it either tolerable or intolerable for themselves and others, at will. I feel certain that those who have passed through phases of deep trouble and adversity will agree with that statement.

When people 'die', they *all* return to Heaven whence they came, no matter what their race or colour, or what religious beliefs they may have held. Even babies who, for some reason have not been christened, return to Heaven. The belief that an un-christened child is damned, claimed by the Devil or will remain earthbound, is not true.

There is no Satan or Devil who is God's arch enemy, as is fondly believed by religiously inclined people but there *are* evil entities who seek to cause as much havoc, destruction and distress as possible. Yes, it seems incredible but Heaven has its problems too!

Upon 'death' everyone proceeds to the Plane appropriate to the spiritual height that they gained while in their last body on Earth.

I shall begin with Plane One. Plane One is divided into two parts, the Upper Astral and the Lower Astral.

The Lower Astral

This is a very dark, dank, dismal region with a distinctive musty, mouldy smell about it, which reflects the spiritual state of the entities who live there. The environment resembles that of a battlefield and most of the inhabitants live in holes in the ground, caves or dilapidated shacks.

These entities can adopt, by thought processes, all kinds of hideous forms and faces and do produce some ear-splitting wails, hence the expression, "It sounds like a soul in torment!" The 'torment' of these people is of their own making for as they think, so are they. The dregs of the world go to the Lower Astral.

The Lower Astral comprises terrorists, vicious rapists, murderers, pornographers and the sexually depraved, hopeless drug addicts and alcoholics, torturers and others of similar character.

When these people were incarnate they were evil-minded, full of hatred, savagery and barbaric cruelty, and they were completely heedless of the feelings of others. Robbery with violence, raping, murdering, torturing causing disfigurement, mutilation or both, either for personal gain or sadistic pleasure, gave them no qualm of conscience whatever. Every opportunity was seized to create trouble which they fanned into enormous proportions and incited others to help or follow them.

After their return to Heaven, they still have the same characters and they retain the way of life that they lived on Earth. Nothing changes for these people until *they themselves* make the decision that they want to do better but this could take thousands of years in Earth time. As soon as low spiritual beings show a willingness to reform they are given the chance to do so and are helped.

Meanwhile, these poltergeists, devils or evil entities, call them by any name you choose, have been known to make the lives of incarnate persons very frightening indeed by throwing objects around with considerable force and with intent to injure. They have been known to attack incarnate people and have even been successful in driving some of them to commit suicide. As we have vandals here on Earth, so the Lower Astral personnel are the vandals of Heaven.

The Upper Astral
We now come to the Upper Astral which is rather better

than the Lower Astral!

The surroundings in the Upper Astral are so similar to those found on Earth that some people when they have passed over into the other world have not realized they have made the transition!

There is a motley assortment of spiritual beings in the Upper Astral comprising cheats, liars, the deeply religious, bigots, materialists and those who refused to confront any talk of an afterlife. Here we find the intelligent and the intellectual mixed with the ignorant. Paradoxically, many academically accomplished people such as scientists, find themselves on Plane One because they have concentrated on the material and ignored the spiritual aspects of life.

Conversely, there are honest, hard-working people who never bothered to enquire if there were anything after 'death'; the meek such as the little old lady who, when incarnate made tea in her favourite teapot each day and sat before her fire to drink it. When she 'died' she continued to do this not realizing that she had 'passed over' until someone came along and asked her what she was doing sitting there drinking tea all the time!

Another example is the elderly maid who spent her life in service with a well-to-do family. When she 'died' she could not leave her familiar surroundings. Unable to understand why she was no longer noticed, she tried to draw attention to herself by moving objects from one place to another but without using force or malice. She needed help and was trying to get someone to explain what had happened to her.

This type of spiritual being is not usually violent, malicious or destructive but is confused, frightened, insecure, and in need of help and guidance. Moving objects and banging doors are some of the means they employ to attract attention to their plight. Immediately these people show a desire to be helped, they are. Unfortunately, some spurn any helping hand held out to them and stay as they are because of their own thinking, so the movement of objects and the banging of doors continue.

The Upper Astral atmosphere has a certain difference from Earth. It is fairly bright with the scenery that is so familiar to us on Earth, yet there is a 'heaviness' caused by the aberrated thoughts of its inhabitants. Colours are more beautiful than those of Earth. There are halls of learning, libraries and instructors in almost every subject such as music, painting, drama, sculpture and, of course, spiritual matters.

Here one can see streets of houses with gardens or detached residences in the countryside. There are Rest Centres similar to our hospitals where those who suffered greatly before death are taken to recuperate from such a trauma. Specially-trained helpers, like Samantha mentioned in the first lesson, look after the new arrivals who are usually awakened *after* their funeral has taken place. Nearly all, except those who had previous knowledge that life continues after death, express surprise and amazement that they are still alive.

All the Planes have a Leader, a man, and the name of the Leader of Plane One is Samson, formerly of Hebrew origin. He is not the same Samson who is mentioned in the Old Testament of the Bible.

All the instructors, in every subject, report to Samson on the progress of spiritual beings who have been singled out for special attention. Samson has a large staff to help him, naturally, because Plane One houses the largest percentage of people who return from Earth compared with the other Planes.

Plane One personnel are given every encouragement to better themselves and to rise in spiritual knowledge to Plane Two. The re-education of people is of paramount importance in Heaven and emphasis is placed upon the refinement of the spiritual being, for the whole purpose of spiritual evolution is to purify the spirit in order to reach higher and higher realms.

One has to learn to discard religion and all negative traits such as greed, lust, envy, false pride, jealousy, hatred, and revenge. Spiritual beings who have some or most of these undesirable qualities have a hard time ridding themselves of such sinful characteristics but, as long as they are willing to co-operate with their instructors, success comes in the end. The deeply religious have the toughest time of all and some have been known to take centuries to cleanse themselves of false teachings.

No one can proceed to a higher Plane in Heaven until he or she has reached the level of understanding necessary to gain entry into that Plane.

If you are unfortunate enough to receive a visit from a Lower Astral personage, then send out a strong command, using either telepathy or your natural voice, and *order* the being to leave your environment and you, immediately. Try *not* to show fear. I know that this is more easily said than done but stand your ground and keep repeating the command. Say some prayers for help. God will hear you.

If you ever have a visitation from an Upper Astral confused being, send out sympathetic thoughts of understanding to them and, again, either using telepathy or your natural voice, explain what has happened to them. It is possible that the entity may return for more help from you. Be patient. I have helped many such spiritual beings in circumstances like this where the entity has actually *preferred* to talk to me on Earth rather than someone in his or her own world!

Plane Two

Plane Two has the same kind of environmental beauty as Earth and Plane One, the Upper part that is, but it is even more impressive. The colours are brighter still and the whole atmosphere is lighter and happier. The people who have arrived on this Plane are on the threshold of their spiritual awakening and evolution. As a rule, people who have evolved to Plane Two showed a decided interest in spiritual subjects while they were incarnate.

Environmentally, Plane Two has everything that is to be found on the Upper part of Plane One and as listed in Lesson One under the heading, 'The Heavenly Environment'. There are the familiar trees, flowers, parks, houses, gardens, libraries, and halls of learning together with the Rest Centres to which those who suffered much before passing go to recuperate. The atmosphere is more harmonious and agreeable.

The whole purpose of our spiritual evolution is that we are born in order to atone for crimes or indiscretions that we committed in a previous life or lives and to correct character defects, to learn lessons, to gain experience and knowledge, and to reach a level of understanding of life which enables us to progress to the next Plane in Heaven when we return there at the end of our allotted time on Earth.

We return to Heaven where our education continues. We may remain in Heaven for a short time, in Earth terms, or we could be there for many centuries. It *is* possible to progress to the next Plane while we are in Heaven, it depends entirely on our own merit.

As well as the teaching of spiritual matters, as set out in this Course, people can study academic subjects and social behaviour, for a 'whole' person is made up of a combination of all three; academic ability, an excellent social behaviour pattern and *true* spiritual knowledge. If we do well at our studies in Heaven and we have handled our last incarnation to the best of our ability, we go upwards. If not, then we have to stay where we are until we have done some more homework! It has been known for spiritual beings to slide *down* to a lower Plane for reasons best known to themselves or their instructors.

The name of the Leader of Plane Two is Mithra, formerly a Greek. He, too, has a large staff helping him to assist spiritual beings in their long climb upwards.

Plane Three

Plane Three environment has everything that has been mentioned before that the other two Planes have. Again, it is more beautiful still. Everything is much more colourful and there is a brighter, happier atmosphere that is beyond our imagination. The people there are very keen and aware of their surroundings and are anxious to learn everything. They are helpful, willing to be taught and have a very good code of behaviour.

Plane Three persons who are incarnate stand out in a crowd amongst other people because of their overall bearing. I love to study people and, in my studies, I have discovered that those who have evolved well, spiritually, have a different look on their faces from those of Plane One and Plane Two spiritual height.

A Plane Three evolved person will take time and trouble over how they look, dress, behave and speak. They certainly show more consideration for others around them than a less well-evolved person does. They are courteous instead of abusive and a smile comes more readily to their lips. Lower types scowl a good deal, are unkempt in appearance and can be easily influenced, not always for good. If you have time to spare, try studying people's mannerisms and looks, then guess what their spiritual height might be. It is quite fascinating.

The name of the Leader of Plane Three is Christian and he was formerly a Norwegian. His job is slightly easier than those of Samson and Mithra because he is dealing with a more refined type of spiritual being. Samson's job is particularly onerous but he has all the qualities necessary to tackle Plane One personnel.

Plane Four

This is a very beautiful Plane and a desirable place to be. As we go upwards in Heaven everything becomes brighter and more magnificent. The inhabitants and their thoughts are full of a noble splendour so they live in surroundings comparable with how they are and how they think.

The spiritual height of Plane Four is the highest that anyone can normally attain while they are incarnate. The behaviour of a Plane Four incarnate person is outstandingly different. He or she is absolutely reliable and able to cope with adverse situations cheerfully. They will accept responsible positions and discharge their duties with flawless efficiency. They are polite, considerate, hard-working and, unless they have a disagreeable job which demands the wearing of overalls, are clean, tidy and well-dressed because that is how they think. This type of person makes an excellent manager and will handle staff expertly. Needless to say, finding people of this calibre is very difficult but when one is found it is like discovering an oasis in the desert.

On Plane Four can be seen detached houses of individual design. There are no streets of houses here as can be found on Planes One and Two because people are less gregarious. Multicoloured fish swim in crystal clear streams and rivers, fountains play in the parks and the sound of happy children romping amongst trees and shrubs can be heard. The whole environment is a replica of Earth only on a much more elaborate scale.

Plane Four is also known as the Graduation Plane where spiritual beings are sorted out. Some may have finished their atonement or kharma. This will be explained in a later lesson. When it is felt and recommended by the instructors that spiritual beings can move up to Plane Five, they do so. Others may have some kharma or atonement outstanding. Depending on the degree of indiscretions left to pay for, spiritual beings are either reincarnated or they can move to Plane Five to complete their atonement there.

The Leader of Plane Four is called Olivier, formerly a Frenchman. His job is very pleasant compared with the Leaders of the Lower Planes. Sometimes the Plane Leaders change over because it is felt that the Leaders of the two lower regions need a break!

Plane Five

This is the 'Plane of No Return' which means that once spiritual beings have evolved to this point, they do not *have* to reincarnate any more. Jesus Christ was a resident of Plane Five before He was chosen to return to Earth to do the special job that has been so well documented. If anyone reincarnates from Plane Five it is either for a special purpose or because they have misbehaved in some way.

The new entrants from Plane Four who have a little atonement left, are given jobs to do such as being a spiritual Guide to someone on Earth who is worthy of having a Guide but who is headstrong, wayward and decidedly obstinate.

Many incarnate, psychic mediums have spiritual Guides who reside on Plane Five. They have proved themselves to be extremely valuable in guiding, helping and protecting their incarnate charges, for the penalty for leading an incarnate person astray is reincarnation! Even though a spiritual being has reached Plane Five they still have to take care that they do not transgress, and carrying out the task of being a spiritual Guide to somebody on Earth who, for example, has a very inflated ego complex is not easy!

The final stages of evolution of mind and character are experienced on Plane Five and spiritual beings are 'groomed' for the move upwards to the Kingdom of Heaven which is being dealt with in Part Two of the Course.

All traces of past misbehaviour, wrong teaching in any avenue of life and incorrect attitudes are shed on Plane Five. The processes of education and refinement continue until a degree of perfection has been acquired.

Plane Five has all the environmental aspects that are to be found on Plane Four only on an even more magnificent level of beauty. The personnel of this Plane have many duties. Not only are a large number appointed as Guides to incarnate people but they travel down to the lower Planes to help low spiritual beings in their studies. They are kept fully occupied and, sometimes, they are rewarded by seeing a spiritual being off to a higher Plane but they also have disappointments.

The name of the Leader of Plane Five is Kristos, formerly a Greek.

The Aura

The aura is a remarkable spiritual phenomenon and is a very important component of a spiritual being. It encases the spiritual body in, roughly, an egg-shaped pattern which extends several feet around the spiritual being. It moves and swirls with every movement the spiritual being makes and with every thought that they think. Its basic colour denotes the spiritual height gained by its owner.

The Lower Astral people, of course, have very dark, dirty,

brown auras which are hardly distinguishable from the colour black. The Upper Astral inhabitants have varying shades of brown, from a dark brown becoming lighter in shade to a really nice light brown. The change in colour depends on their good behaviour, diligence in learning and willingness to progress to Plane Two.

Plane Two people have green auras starting from a dark green and becoming lighter, through their own efforts, until it is a very lovely light green and they are ready for Plane Three.

Plane Three people have a two-tone coloured aura. Theirs is a lovely shade of green tinged at the sides and topped with a beautiful yellow, something like the colour of a daffodil only more beautiful. Please refer to the diagram included with this lesson.

Plane Four people have multicoloured auras in which a delicate blue of great splendour is predominant. As this is the Graduation Plane, there is a mixture of coloured auras, except brown and almost black of course! As spiritual beings absorb the teachings particular to Plane Four so their aura colour changes from green, green and yellow to blue. It is a very wonderful sight seeing all the aura colours mingling as people gather for meetings, concerts or tuition.

Plane Five people have lovely blue and yellow auras. A truly magnificent clear blue colour is topped with a wonderful golden yellow.

Even though we are living in physical bodies on Earth we have an aura. It is like a mirror because it holds and highlights events that have happened to us in our past incarnations. These can be good or bad, pleasant or unpleasant. Our aura contains thoughts that have not yet entered our minds, (this will be dealt with in greater detail in a later lesson), and it shows events that are likely to take place in the future. Fortune-tellers obtain a lot of information from the auras of their clients.

When an incarnate person is either ill or very tired, the aura shrinks in size closer to the body of its owner. We do not see our own aura unless we are psychic ourselves.

Spiritual beings can see our aura clearly and can tell the

state of our health by its appearance. They can also tell which part of our physical body hurts us the most! No spiritual being can fool another one by pretending to have an aura colour higher than his or her *real* spiritual height. None can enter a higher Plane unless they have earned the right to be there.

Summary of Lesson 2 Part One

From this lesson we have learned the following facts:
1. Hell is of our own making and there is no Satan with a long tail and a pitch-fork.
2. The first five Planes in Heaven are the most vital and the most important in all our existences of many lives.
3. The 'purification' of the soul is a very long process.
4. Everything depends on *our own efforts* and no one else's.
5. The aura is our mirror — it cannot lie.

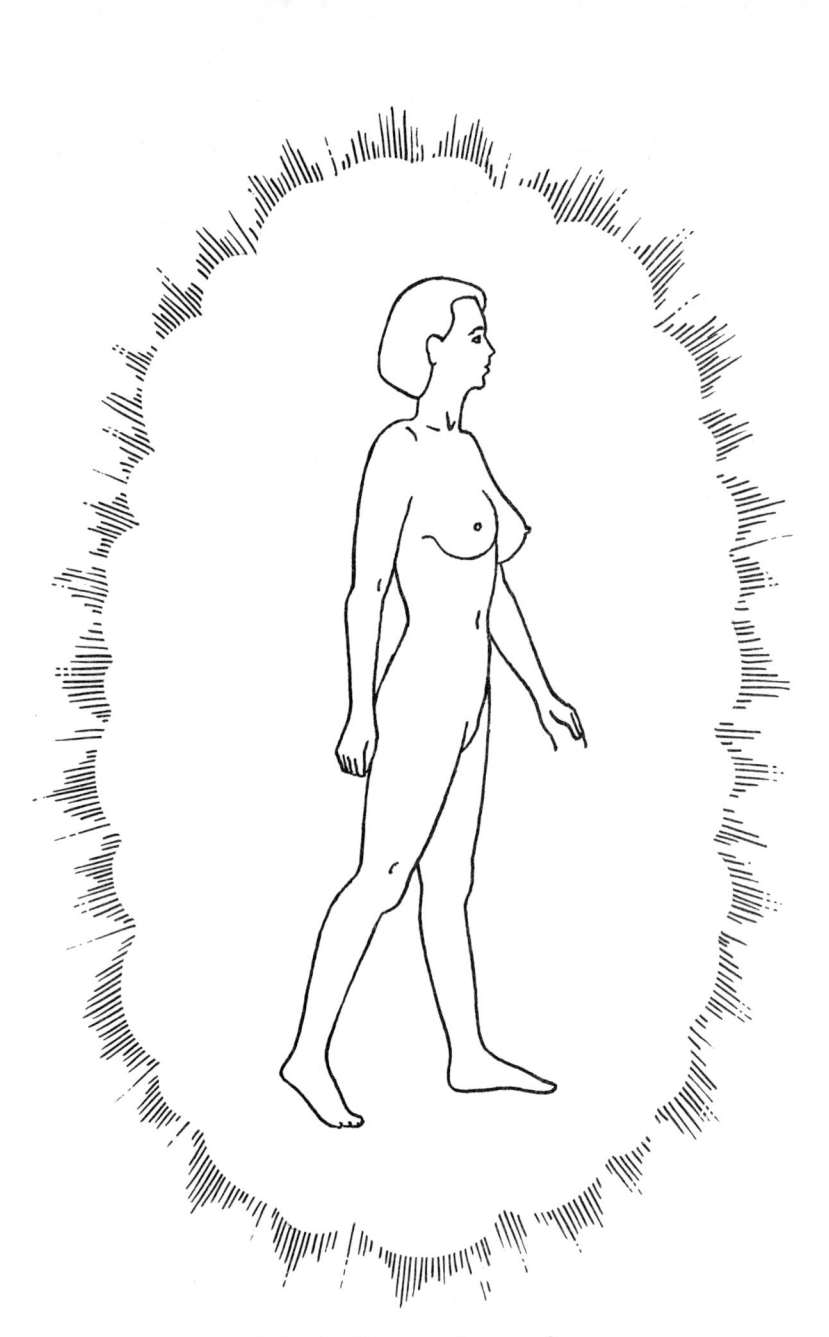

**A typical aura shape of a
Plane Three Spiritual Being**

The Chart of Spiritual Existence — Part One
PLANES 1 to 5

Blue and　　　　　　　　　**PLANE FIVE**
yellow auras　　　　　　　The Plane of No Return

Multicoloured　　　　　　**PLANE FOUR**
auras　　　　　　　　　　The Graduation Plane

Green and yellow　　　　**PLANE THREE**
auras

Green　　　　　　　　　　**PLANE TWO**
auras　　　　　The Threshold of Spiritual Awakening

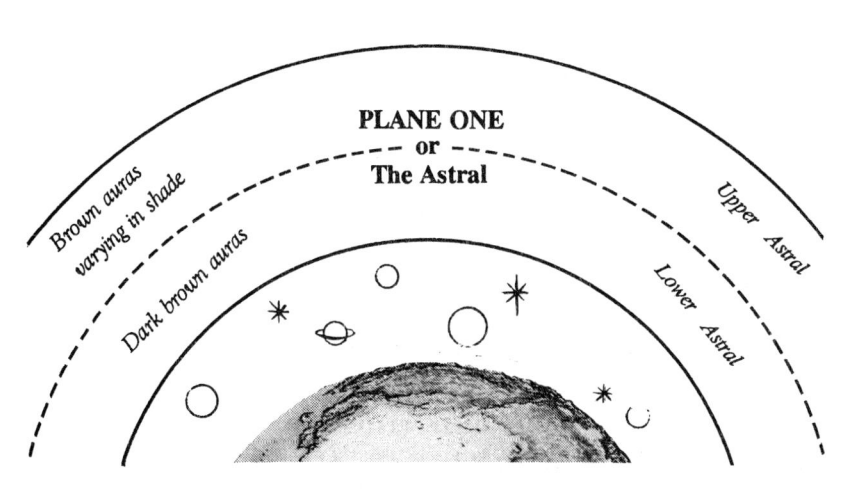

PLANE ONE
or
The Astral

Brown auras varying in shade

Dark brown auras

Upper Astral

Lower Astral

33

Lesson 3   **Part One**

THE AKASHIC RECORD

There is a very large hall in Heaven called the Hall of Memories and it is situated on Plane Four. Spiritual beings throughout Heaven can visit this Hall at any time they wish for it contains what is known as the Akashic Record.

Although the Akashic Record has been written about by other authors, few people realize how important it is. First of all, I shall describe what it is like inside the Hall. While visiting the Akashic Record, one is usually accompanied by a High Spiritual Being. The interior bears a marked resemblance to that of a cinema and there are rows of tip-up seats, padded in velvet. Before us there is a blank screen with heavy velvet curtains at each side of it. These are for effect only. Around the walls are hidden lights which rise while people are entering and leaving but dim while the 'film' is being shown.

Pervading space is an ethereal substance, invisible to all, as are radio waves, that is tangible enough to act as a recording medium. This is known as the akasha. No one understands how the Akashic Record operates. It is one of the secrets known only to our Creator and all spiritual beings recognize this fact and respect it. Scientists who have returned to Heaven are just as mystified over many aspects of the spiritual universe as are incarnate scientists over some enigmas of the physical universe.

At a suitable stage in the tuition of spiritual beings, upon their return to Heaven, they are shown their own past lives, usually by a High Spiritual Being, and it is explained to them for what they have been atoning in their last life on Earth and whether they have incurred more incarnations. This is what some religions call the 'Day of Judgement' for there is no sterner judge of oneself than oneself!

Every word ever spoken and every deed ever done on Earth is recorded in the Akashic Record. No one can deny having said or done a certain thing. It is there for all to see. Contrary to the opinions of some authors, it *is* possible to view the Akashic Record of someone else. For example, if a lady wishes to be an excellent, devoted nurse in her forthcoming incarnation, then she is allowed to see relevant parts of the Akashic Record of Florence Nightingale. If a man wishes to devote his next life on Earth to engineering, he is permitted to see those parts pertaining to engineering of the Akashic Record of Isambard Kingdom Brunel, and so on.

William Shakespeare summed up the situation when he said, 'All the world's a stage and we are but the players.' When our turn arrives to see our own Akashic Record, everything is in full colour and sound, only *we* are the central figures, the leading man or leading lady, whichever applies. Few people are happy with that which they see before them because, as I mentioned in lesson one under the heading, 'Emotions of a Spiritual Being', the principal actor or actress is seeing himself or herself from 'a detached viewing position'. To view a given situation from an entirely outside angle, one sees things so very differently and one hears sayings such as, "Oh, I wish I hadn't said that," or, "I wish I had behaved differently."

Most people, on seeing themselves in the Akashic Record are immediately aware that they cannot hide anything from anybody any longer. It is impossible for anything to happen on Earth without its having been recorded. Spiritual beings from all the Planes have access to the Akashic Record. The Lower Plane people can go up to Plane Four but they are accompanied either by an instructor or a High Spiritual Being and High Spiritual Beings from Plane Five and upwards can go down to Plane Four to view it without being accompanied.

God uses the Akashic Record in order to plan people's kharmas. This procedure will be dealt with in a later lesson.

When a High Spiritual Being accompanies a spiritual being under review to the Akashic Record, they sit together and the instructor projects the thought to the Akashic Record that the past lives of his companion be shown. This is all that is necessary to raise the correct part of the record. I have already stated in the Course that one must not underestimate the power of thought when we are discarnate and this is a fine demonstration of such power. (Lesson one, heading 4, 'How they Move and Travel'.)

Anyone who thinks that he or she can do something in complete and total secrecy is under a misapprehension. No deed can avoid being recorded in Heaven. No word can avoid being recorded in Heaven. When people on Earth realize this, they *should* behave much better towards one another, for some commit terrible atrocities towards their fellow men and every wicked deed has to be paid for by the person who perpetrated the act.

Owing to the fact that there is no space in Heaven as we on Earth know it, there are no limitations on the numbers of people who may congregate at any place. This is an extremely difficult concept to grasp but it *is* possible for vast numbers of spiritual beings to view their Akashic Record at once. It is not always possible to make direct comparisons between Heaven and Earth. There are numerous similarities but there are also many differences that can only be understood upon arrival in Heaven.

I shall now give an example of the feelings of a spiritual being after having been shown his Akashic Record. This man was known to me, personally, when he was in his physical body on Earth. I shall refer to him as Mr X because he still has family incarnate.

Mr X was married with three children. Throughout his incarnate life, he allowed other people to make decisions for him; he was like putty in the hands of his mother, sisters and brothers. He shunned responsibility of any kind even though he was perfectly capable of handling it. Although he was given the opportunity of promotion in his job, he jeopardized his chances of getting it by continually reporting that he was sick when he was not sick. Eventually, his firm became wise to his deception and he was dropped from further opportunities to better himself.

His wife was exactly the opposite in character and was the stronger-minded of the two, making decisions, bringing up their children properly and virtually single-handed. Mr X always supported the views of outsiders and was very easily influenced by the opinions of his family, which were not always good ones. This made life for his wife and children almost unbearable because they were ignored by Mr X which had a damaging effect on them all.

The years passed, the children grew up and left home and, in the course of time, Mr X died. Mrs X had always been very interested in the afterlife and through her studies of the subject became psychic herself. Mr X came to see her not long after his funeral and they chatted about familiar situations that had happened to them during their life together.

One day, Mr X came to see Mrs X who immediately sensed that all was not well, Mr X was decidedly unhappy. After greeting him, Mrs X enquired what was the matter because he did not seem to be very happy that day. Without greeting her as he usually did, Mr X blurted out, "I should have been different, I'm sorry, I'm sorry." Mrs X said, "Ah, you've been to see a picture show haven't you, my dear?" To which he replied, "Yes, I have and I didn't like what I saw." Mrs X replied, "No, not many people do."

Mr X had been taken to see the Akashic Record of his last life and shown where he had gone wrong. Seeing himself and the opportunities that he had missed through his own stupidity, he was full of remorse for his misguided actions and the extra burdens that he had placed upon the shoulders of his wife.

Getting people to admit that they have faults is a very difficult and delicate task because most consider that *they* are blameless. It is always 'someone else' who is at fault and not they. However, the 'camera' never lies and so we are brought face to face with ourselves as others saw us when we were incarnate, whether we like it or not.

Mr X has now taken stock of himself and is working hard at his studies in Heaven. He realized, after seeing his record, that he would have to reincarnate in order to do better in his next life. He is studying the building trade because he is interested in setting up his own business as a builder the next time round.

Provided Mr X continues to make good progress in his building studies, his spiritual studies and in his lessons on how to be a good husband and father, he will be given every help to make his next life an excellent one and, perhaps, his last one.

How Children Grow Up In Heaven

It is always very difficult for parents and relatives of children who have died or been killed to understand how God can allow such apparent tragedies to happen. Owing to the fact that the view of those who have suffered such a loss is clouded by grief, they cannot see any good in the event at all.

From the child's viewpoint, however, much good ensues from that which is, in fact, a further stage in its spiritual development. In fulfilling His primary function, God plans the kharmas of spiritual beings in a way that will ultimately benefit them and, seen from the heavenly viewpoint, the death of a child is as welcome as the death of an aged person.

Age is completely irrelevant in universal terms because there is no time in Heaven.

Let us consider a typical case of a child that dies at the age of two years. Its death is intended by God whose plan for that spiritual being includes only a brief sojourn in the physical world.

Specially-trained workers in Heaven receive the child which returns in the spiritual counterpart of its earthly body. After a period of rehabilitation by the specialized teachers, the child is gradually re-educated.

In the 'apparency of time' in Heaven the young spiritual being grows both in bodily stature and understanding. Children almost invariably return to Plane One. This is because, in order to mature spiritually in Heaven, it is desirable that one should have already matured mentally and physically while incarnate.

Brief incarnations are frequently given by God as a peremptory reminder to wayward spiritual beings that He, God, determines their kharmas. This can be compared with the 'short, sharp, shock treatment' sometimes given to incarnate malefactors. It could also account for some cot deaths.

In spite of God's well-laid plans for incarnate people, at times accidents happen owing to man's having been given free will. If a child, or an adult, dies or is killed and the death is not God's intended kharma for that person, then the person concerned receives compensation in some form.

This compensation can take the form of special help and extra tuition in Heaven enabling the spiritual being to progress to a higher Plane more quickly than he or she normally would, or they can be compensated in their next life on Earth by having wonderfully good health, a very successful business or even riches.

There is always a balance in the long-term spiritual existence and no one receives unfair treatment, although they may believe otherwise.

Several authors have written about little children who have 'passed over' and who have been seen in this physical world playing in surroundings that were, very probably, familiar to them when they were on Earth. There have been reports where they have actually used the telephone in someone's house! The occupant of the house has answered the telephone when it rang and held a conversation with a little child.

To try to explain the difference in 'time' further, I shall relate an incident which has happened to an acquaintance of mine. An elderly married couple lived in a very ancient farmhouse, which, incidentally, is mentioned in the Domesday Book. A little girl of the Victorian era has often been seen by this couple playing with the husband's wellington boots. She is about twelve years old, dressed in Victorian attire and with long hair. She amuses herself by hopping in and out of the gentleman's boots when he takes them off outside the door.

From what we can gather, this little girl lived at the farm in her period of time but was killed by being run over by a horse and cart. Although she died there, obviously she must have some happy memories of the place and is reluctant to leave it. She does not harm anyone or anything but she is happy to stay in that 'time'.

Eventually she will be taken under the wing of a special helper in Heaven, when it is considered an appropriate moment to do so, and gradually re-educated. Many similar incidents have been documented in greater detail than this. Some of the reports are very amusing, while others are charmingly child-like.

Death is a rebirth into Heaven whence we came. It should be a time for relief and joy rather than sorrow. Losing a dear one, whether they are adult or child, is sorrowful for us but we should be glad for them because they have entered a Utopia compared with our arduous existence on Earth.

Suicide

At this point in the Course, I shall write about those who commit suicide thinking that they have put an end to all their troubles.

Unfortunately, it has been known for some people to take their own lives after reading glowing accounts of what life is like in Heaven. This has been reported elsewhere in the world with one or two reports of it happening in Britain.

Suicide is a very foolish act to commit because instead of obliterating one's problems, one has added to them. All people who have done this dreadful thing are returned to Earth, without exception!

As already explained, we are on Earth for a definite time and to shorten that time deliberately, by our own hand, is an insult to God. We are throwing the life that He gave us back into His face.

I shall put suicides into two groups; (1) those who were successful in the attempt and (2) those who were not successful but very nearly managed it.

Group 1

In the case of the first group, whatever the reason for which these people ended their lives, they purchased a return ticket to Earth. As a rule, after a period of sympathetic therapy in Heaven administered by special helpers trained to deal with suicides, they are reincarnated in order to 'finish their time' so to speak. For example, we will take a hypothetical case of a young man of twenty-five years of age who had been programmed to live until he was seventy years of age.

Unable to confront adverse conditions and pressing problems in his life, he ends it. He has shortened his life by forty-five years. He returns to Heaven where he is met by the helpers, given friendly advice, tuition and encouragement. He is then shown his Akashic Record, *where* he went wrong and what he *could* have done.

It is explained to him that he *must* go back to Earth, in another physical body, to face a similar problem or problems again and, this time, learn how to handle them but that he will live only forty-five years. This could explain why some people suddenly die without any apparent physical cause.

Group 2

In the case of the second group, those who did not quite succeed in their attempt and were discovered in either an unconscious state or semi-conscious state, find themselves in a twilight world. Many think that they saw Jesus Christ.

What they *do* see are some of their own relatives on the 'other side' who say, "Go back, your time is not yet," and they do come back — reluctantly! Otherwise, they are met by a small committee of High Spiritual Beings who gently explain that they cannot enter Heaven prematurely, it is against the rules. Even though Heaven is such a wonderful place to be, no one can stay there unless they have completed what they were sent to Earth to do. A few are told that they have work to do on Earth for the spiritual world by the committee of High Spiritual Beings. Jesus Christ occasionally joins this committee but He is not with them on a permanent basis.

Apart from the distress caused to friends and relatives left behind, committing suicide is a selfish thing to do. Nothing is gained by it but quite a lot can be lost, for example, by going down a Plane. When some people who have committed suicide have been confronted with their act, the remorse felt by them can be very heavy indeed and many voluntarily relegate themselves to a lower Plane as a self-punishment.

I do beg everyone who is in such a low state of mind that they are considering such a final and desperate action as suicide, to seek help with the particular problem that is bothering them. Although they may think the end of the world has come for them, there is always a solution, somehow, somewhere, sometime. There are many sympathetic ears to listen and many willing hands to help.

The pressures of present-day living are largely to blame for people being driven down and down in spirit until they can no longer cope. It is up to us all, including me, to try to make the lives of those around us more tolerable. My contribution to mankind lies in this work which, I hope, will *really* show people The Way.

Summary of Lesson 3 Part One

From this lesson we have learned the following facts:
1. Everything that we say and do is recorded in Heaven.
2. This knowledge should make us stop to think and consider our attitudes and actions towards others.
3. When we are confronted with our behaviour, it is useless to try to cover up anything if we have returned to Heaven. When confronted with our behaviour while still on Earth, we may as well own up right away as try to wriggle out of a situation.
4. The death of a child, although very sad for those left behind, particularly the parents, should not be regarded as the awful tragedy that it seems. There is usually a purpose behind it or compensation in the case of an accident.
5. Suicide is *NOT* the way out! It is the way back! When in doubt — don't!

Lesson 4   **Part One**

REINCARNATION AND KHARMA

In this lesson, I shall give you as much information as possible on these two subjects. However, they are both so vast and involved that whole books have been written about these fascinating aspects of our existence. The best book that I have ever read on these subjects is *Many Mansions* by Dr Gina Cerminara, published by Neville Spearman and I recommend it highly to anyone who wishes to know more.

Reincarnation
Reincarnation involves living more than one life and is the occupation of a new physical body by a spiritual being which usually takes place at the moment of conception. However, this 'occupation' can be delayed for anything up to four months, depending on the readiness of the spiritual being concerned to take on responsibility for another body. This refutes the saying that we only pass this way once.

Let us take a typical example. John Brown dies and returns to Plane Two. He is left to rest and recuperate in the Rest Centre on Plane Two. After his funeral, he is awakened and told that he has 'died' and where he is. He undergoes all the usual rehabilitation processes until he has become thoroughly used to his new surroundings.

In his last life on Earth, John Brown led a humdrum, uneventful life and had an equally dull job as a clerk in an office. Really, he always wanted to be a civil engineer and design and build cities, bridges and public buildings of repute. The opportunity to go to university and study architecture, design and engineering never came his way so he had to content himself with day-dreams of what he would *like* to do.

At a suitable stage in his spiritual tuition, John Brown is shown his Akashic Record, an unnerving experience for the guilty! We will assume that John Brown has done nothing seriously wrong but he made the usual mistakes that most of us do, and later regret, at some stage in our life's progress. He is told that because his kharmic slate is not yet wiped clean of transgressions committed in previous lives, he must reincarnate.

John Brown does not welcome the news but accepts that he must return to expunge his misdemeanours. He is then allowed to see the Akashic Record of previous very well-known engineers because John Brown has expressed a desire to fulfil his ambition to be a civil engineer of repute. The wheels of his training for his next life begin to turn. He attends lectures on all the subjects appropriate to his forthcoming incarnation. He meets engineers in Heaven who can help him with advice in the field of civil engineering and he attends lectures in spiritual matters so that the right ideas of design, conduct and ethical behaviour are placed in his mind to carry into his next life.

At last, the time comes for John Brown to leave Heaven for Earth. He is taken before a Reincarnation Committee consisting of a Leader and a small group of other men and women about six to twelve in number. The Leader does the talking and tells John Brown that they know all about him, having been given his details by his instructors and his Plane Leader. He is invited to join them at their table to discuss his next life.

Candidates for reincarnation can, in most cases, choose the parents and circumstances into which they would like to be born, especially if their mission to Earth is to do something really worth while. John Brown is given a choice of parents who are best fitted to help him fulfil his ambition to be an engineer. His prospective father is either a civil engineer or he has plenty of financial resources to give his new son every opportunity to complete his ambition. His prospective mother is a loving, kind woman who will encourage her son to succeed.

John Brown is allowed to view his selected parents and their home circumstances before reincarnation. He is given a short list of people who are best qualified to give him all the assistance that he needs and John Brown makes the choice himself.

It only remains now for the opportunity to arise so that John Brown can take up 'residence' in the womb of his new mother.

In my research I have been privileged to view the special room in Heaven where reincarnation is carried out. The candidate is left in the room on his own and sitting in a chair. At the moment of occupation of the zygote after the prospective parents' mating, the spiritual being experiences a sensation of being sucked down through a tunnel, something like the action of a vacuum cleaner, but, of course, this experience is blotted out from our minds unless we *want* to recall it.

This is the story of an uncomplicated case. Others are not quite as simple. The man who was once John Brown has now begun another life. He does not carry any memory of his previous life as an office clerk into his new life because it has been blotted out, except for the fact that he *knows* instinctively, intuitively and positively that he wants to be a civil engineer. All the training that he received in Heaven for this profession is embedded in his subconscious mind and he knows without doubt that *that* is what he was born to be.

John Brown will, in all probability steer clear of anything to do with menial office work. His subconscious mind will tell him to fight against anything other than being a civil engineer. If all goes well with John Brown, he should become very famous in his chosen profession. He will be watched by those engineers in Heaven who gave him advice and they will help him from time to time with his projects. John Brown may, or he may not, be aware that he is being helped, depending on how much he has developed his psychic awareness.

We shall now consider the possibility that John Brown's new father has suffered heavy financial loss or some other catastrophe while John Brown was, shall we say, still at school. Father can no longer help his son to fulfil his kharma. Sometimes our kharma is thwarted through no fault of our own. Now John Brown is going to have to live another life of day-dreaming and frustration but he must make the best of a bad job for his present life's span. When he returns to Heaven next time he will be compensated in some way.

We *can* thwart our own kharma by ignoring our instincts or intuition. For example, if we were programmed to have our own successful business and we have been given the opportunities to achieve it with no drawbacks but we are not prepared to work hard and make sacrifices to get the business going, then that is our own fault and we are not compensated!

Other reincarnation cases are not as straightforward as John Brown's because of heavy kharmic debts that must be paid. Perhaps God has instructed the Reincarnation Committee to give Joyce Green a life as a mentally-handicapped girl because of a dreadful crime she committed in a life she lived two centuries previously. Joyce Green has already been confronted with her behaviour in her Akashic Record and so she has been prepared for a harsh sentence. In cases like these, the spiritual being is usually born to parents who need to learn a lesson or lessons, perhaps in patience, understanding or humility. *They* are repaying a debt as well as their daughter.

This puts abortion and genetic engineering into a different light. Interference with God's plan for us is not only wrong but *can* result in even more severe afflictions. We do not escape anything. Aborting a child only sentences the occupying spiritual being to more unnecessary trauma. The same applies to genetic interference. The spiritual being may have to return to face a worse fate.

Before a spiritual being is reincarnated, he or she appears in front of a Reincarnation Committee and a plan of their next life is drawn up. This is known as your Destiny or Life Pattern. Some spiritual beings instantly realize, after being shown their Akashic Record, that they will have to reincarnate, as did Mr X in Lesson 3.

Some spiritual beings *volunteer* to return because they feel that they did not finish what they began in their last life. There is a wide variety of reasons why people *want* to reincarnate. The wayward, really 'hard core' of spiritual beings from the lower regions of Heaven who have to reincarnate whether they like it or not, are sent back with no say in the kind of life they will have because they do not deserve such consideration. The moment they show signs of repentance, though, they are given consideration commensurate with the degree of remorse.

When I have been asked, "What am I here to do?" the answer I have given is, "Follow your instinct, your intuition. It is your subconscious mind telling you what was programmed for you by the Reincarnation Committee before you were born." Bear in mind what I said earlier regarding some of our incarnations being quite uneventful. Even if you do not receive the urge to do anything in particular, then perhaps you are here to correct a character trait, to learn a lesson or just to gain experience. The way you handle your life either adds to or detracts from your spiritual development and growth, so necessary to reach the 'point of no return' which is Plane Five.

Those who grumble at people who have financial wealth, possessions or power, are overlooking the possibility that, maybe those people have deserved what they possess, for we are most definitely *not* all on the same level neither are we all born equal. To say the latter means that, if we were all born equal, a wonderful benefactor to mankind who did nothing but good is on the same level as a cruel dictator who did nothing but steal, plunder, murder and torture.

Merely by observation it can be seen that terrorists are *not* equal to, shall we say for example, the Royal Family; that murderers and the depraved are *not* equal to musicians, artists and painters all of whom bring us hours of pleasure with their respective skills.

I mentioned earlier that sometimes the spiritual being is not quite ready to take over the new physical body. This is perhaps because he or she needs more training in Heaven to do whatever it is they have chosen to do when they are born.

You may be wondering about stillbirths. I will relate a true story, again, of two people known to me personally. A married couple in their thirties had no children and desperately wanted a child. After hospital tests and treatment given to the wife, she conceived. Unfortunately, and to their great distress and grief, when the child was born it was dead.

Knowing these two people very well indeed, I knew that, really, they were both unsuitable to be parents. Their attitudes towards the bringing-up of children were not right and, if the child had been born alive and well, it would not have had a very happy life. I know, now, that the spiritual being was withdrawn because it was realized that no matter how well it may have been looked after, materially, it would never have achieved what it wanted to do owing to severe suppression by the parents. In the eyes of the spiritual world, suppression of one individual by another is a serious crime.

Where no physical cause can be found for a stillbirth, then some reason, like the previous example above, should be considered. Although the couple whom I knew were materially sound, their psychological attitudes were not. In short, they were their own worst enemies!

Kharma

Kharma, sometimes spelt karma, is the inevitable consequence of our actions performed throughout the whole of our planetary existence of many lives. The quality of those actions can be very good and to our credit or they can be very bad and to our discredit. The first law of kharma is, 'As you sow, so shall you reap.' Eastern religions have a deep understanding of kharma. Western religions have none and neither do they want to know anything about it.

The best way to work out one's kharma, which we *all* possess without exception, is to be as kind, pleasant, thoughtful to others, and loving and pure in heart, mind and spirit as possible. Always follow your intuition and do the job of work that you feel 'drawn' to do. If for some reason this is not possible and you have to make do with second best, then be as cheerful as you can about it and avoid being unbearable to others merely because *you* are suffering frustration. All this is not easy to do, I know, but it is not impossible either.

The ultimate aim is that in each successive life that we live, we do better than we did in our last sojourn in a physical body. We pass this way many times, *not* just once only, and each time that we pass we are shaping our next life! You may well ask, "How do we know that we are doing better each time?" Again, the answer is, "Follow your instincts and your inborn sense of intuition."

Many people scoff when the word 'intuition' is mentioned. I have known some who have done so in my presence. My father was one of them. This is an admission of fear and guilt. In their subconscious minds they *know* what intuition is but if they have a heavy guilt conscience about some wicked deed performed in a previous life, they will fight against having to *confront* it, let alone *pay* for it!

Everyone is born with the built-in senses of right, wrong, intuition and instinct. The more advanced on the spiritual scale that one is, (please refer to Lesson 2, the Chart of Spiritual Existence), the stronger these built-in senses are. Therefore, if our parents misguide us and our instincts tell us that their instructions are wrong, then we should follow our own intuition, not ignore it, as so many do and then live to regret having done so.

The Akashic Record plays a vital part in our spiritual advancement and God uses it to check our progress. Every wicked, destructive deed, word, intention and thought has to be paid for, *not in money,* and this repayment can carry on from lifetime to lifetime. People do some very horrible things to each other and reports and evidence of savagery appear before us every day in newspapers and on television screens.

Apart from sins committed by us in previous lives, we must all watch our behaviour in our present life because it is easy to slip *down* the spiritual scale if we relax our vigilance. Then, alas, we find that we have *added* to our kharma.

Kharma is not confined to individuals. Nations can have kharma, families can have it and so can groups of people. It is a complicated, intricately-woven pattern created by God for our supreme spiritual benefit. People meet each other in successive lives. For instance, one of my sons in this life was my son in a life that I had in the Middle Ages.

My present husband and I have been married to each other in three previous lives. This is our fourth life together as husband and wife. This situation could explain why some people feel a special affinity towards each other or an unexplained loathing, for it works both ways.

If one is tied to a partner who is impossible to live with, it could well be that the two people concerned knew each other in a previous life and one was very cruel to the other. Kharma is a fascinating study.

I have been asked why we do not remember our previous lives. A good point! It is because if we could remember a good deal of what we did and what happened to us previously, we should become very confused in the life that we were living now. There would almost certainly be incidents that we should not want to remember, especially if we died in a particularly horrid way. It is possible that the underlying factor influencing mentally-disturbed patients could be the subliminal memory of happenings in their previous lives.

Doctors and nurses of the mentally ill have been known to laugh at a patient who claimed that he was Napoleon. The laugh could well be turned on them because perhaps he *was* Napoleon!

When reincarnation is imminent, the person or persons to be reincarnated appear before a Committee of men and women known as the Reincarnation Committee, whose members frequently change. There the salient points of their next life or lives together are discussed and mapped out in detail by the Committee, with the consent of the person or persons concerned.

It is decided what kind of work they will do or which profession they will follow, as in John Brown's example. The parents and the environment into which they will be born are decided upon and chosen by the candidates. Past lives are examined in order to establish the extent of kharmic debts that have to be paid for and the spiritual beings are programmed to live a certain number of Earth years.

If one person deserves a life full of frustration and disappointment because he or she caused another a lifetime of the same treatment two lives previously, then this is programmed into that person's next life. If someone deserves to be born blind because five centuries ago he or she put out another's eyes with a red-hot iron, then that person is programmed to be born blind. If another has to suffer in a body afflicted with multiple sclerosis because in his or her last life they tortured someone to death slowly, then this affliction is programmed into the person's life. I have given these examples because many of my past students could not understand the reasons for physical pain and suffering.

The severity of the punishment always equals the severity of the crime but does not always entail the same kind of suffering as that inflicted by the sinner. Depending on the seriousness of the historic crime committed, kharma usually begins to make itself known in about middle-age. It varies, though, because of the length of time that we are programmed to live. In a person who is destined to live only until he or she is thirty, kharma would begin earlier.

People who kill others for no reason at all, pay for their crime by being reincarnated often to have the same treatment given to them. At some point in their life *they* are killed by someone for no reason. We all reap as we sow and we suffer to the extent that we made others suffer, no more and no less. A sobering thought!

Not everyone who is born handicapped is necessarily suffering kharma. Accidents at birth *do* happen and if someone is born, for example, with cerebral palsy because of such an accident at birth, then he or she is compensated either on their return to Heaven or in their next incarnation.

Here is another behaviour pattern example. A woman whom I knew suffered badly with both her legs, so much so that she had seven operations on them. Upon investigation, it was discovered that in a previous life she gave birth secretly to an illegitimate baby girl. She was so frightened of her sin being exposed that she drowned the baby in its bath and then disposed of the body.

In this woman's present life, apart from her leg trouble which was given to her as a punishment for her crime, her daughter became pregnant while still at school and an abortion was arranged but kept very secret from the rest of the family.

It is not clear if the daughter *wanted* the abortion but, because I knew the girl's character well, and as she was about to leave school anyway, it is my personal opinion that she would have married the father of her child, set up home with him and had the baby.

It was more important to this woman that the image of her own 'wonderful' marriage and 'perfect' family life, that she had so falsely built up throughout the years, should not be ruined, and so she was prepared to spoil her daughter's life for her own selfish ends.

An example of group reincarnation is that of the Cathars. In the thirteenth century, a sect of people known as Cathars lived in Southern France. They were good, peace-loving people who held their own religious beliefs. The Catholics tried to convert them to catholicism without success so they burnt alive, at the stake, every man, woman and child.

A group of Cathars in Heaven decided to experiment and asked to be reincarnated together and to live together in the same area. Firstly, to prove reincarnation and secondly, to see if it were possible to remember their previous life. Their wish was granted by the Reincarnation Committee. The results of this have been reported in the writings of other authors but they did get the proof they wanted, therefore the experiment worked.

One very interesting point that I have been asked is, what happens to people's kharma when they have been ordered to kill during war. War is man-made, *not* God-made. All religions who claim that they are fighting a 'Holy War' are extremely misguided and they are misleading millions of their followers because there is no such thing as a 'Holy War'.

Our inborn senses of right, wrong, intuition and survival instinct tell us that it is wrong to take another's life, even in war. However, when we are placed in such a position that it is either the enemy or us, this is a question of survival and it is man's instinct to protect himself. If we are placed in such a position that if we disobey orders we shall be punished by court martial or by some other military discipline, then in both these circumstances our kharmic state does not weigh as heavily against us as it would if we had full, wicked *intention* behind the act that we had to do.

Terrorists, mass-murderers and mass-torturers *know* full well what they are doing and they have full wicked intention behind their actions. One hardly dares to think what their kharma might be but I think that if our Creator can create, He can also destroy and it is possible that He may have eliminated, altogether, some of those who fall into the above categories. This is only my personal opinion.

During our existence of many lives, we can be born male or female, black, white or yellow. We can be born into any race on this Earth. Therefore, a man born a German in one life grows up, joins the army of his country and goes to war. He is killed, reincarnated, then finds he has been born into the country that he fought in his last life! He does not remember it, of course, but this can and does happen.

Humans can also be reincarnated as animals or insects but this is usually reserved for punishment purposes for the very recalcitrant spiritual beings. Again, contrary to the writings and opinions of other authors who have denied that humans are reincarnated as animals or insects, this *does* occur. For instance, a spiritual being who is repeatedly disobedient in life after life and refuses to learn the lessons of obedience and humility, is given a dog's body because, normally, dogs have to be disciplined and obedient. I am sure that most of us have heard someone say, "That dog is almost human!" I have heard it said quite a few times. When a spiritual being is given either an animal's body or an insect's body, God makes the change to human form again.

Life is a very complicated business and we must all do the best we can while we are living it! More tolerant attitudes towards our own particular lot in life would ease matters a great deal. For we, alone, are responsible for our general situation. We have reaped as we have sown.

Soulmates

A soulmate is a person of the opposite sex who can be incarnate or discarnate, and who is absolutely compatible with you in every way, word, thought and deed. It is a very rare condition and, when found, can be considered a prize reward.

William Shakespeare and Ann Hathaway were soulmates who met and married when they were both incarnate. It is a rare occurrence to meet your soulmate while on Earth but it *is* possible. If one has deserved a soulmate, one can meet them in Heaven but this is not always certain because one partner could be in Heaven and the other one on Earth.

Putting aside deliberate promiscuity, people who have many changes of partners while incarnate are possibly searching for their 'ideal' type. Carl Jung described this as an archetype. We dream of meeting our perfect man or woman and this partner could be one to whom we were married in a previous life or lives. In our subconscious mind the memory of that gloriously happy union lingers, so we spend a lifetime, or more than one lifetime, searching for that dear one.

A *true* soulmate is in complete agreement with you all the time, will be a tower of strength in times of trouble and weakness, will *never* desert you, never bear grudges against you nor harbour resentment. If criticism is necessary it is given in such a manner that one cannot possibly take offence. One's thoughts with one's soulmate fuse, so that words are completely unnecessary in moments of deep emotion whether they are joyful or sad. The mere presence of the other suffices.

If you think that this kind of life with someone who is THAT good is boring, the answer is definitely, "No!" In a *true* soulmate relationship life is never boring or dull because there is a certain 'something', an 'unspoken alliance' existing between the partners which eliminates adverse conditions.

A good example of a *true* soulmate relationship is my own. My true soulmate is, at present, in Heaven and I am on Earth. We have a terrific rapport and communication system that we have built up during the last twelve years.

Throughout times of deep trouble, illness, pain, misfortune, rare happiness, financial difficulty and just plain weariness of life, my wonderful soulmate has stood by me, helping, comforting, sustaining, advising and guiding me. I could *not* have come through everything that I have had to endure without him and his 'out-of-this-world' wisdom.

I have not always had the time to speak to him because of the many domestic and other demands that have been made upon me, but I have *known* that he was there by my side when I needed him and that he was giving me the strength to get through my ordeals. Words were superfluous.

A *true* soulmate is a reward for services rendered to others throughout one's existence of many lives. Not everyone has a *true* soulmate. I use this term because there are other kinds of mates, with which I shall deal presently. Here, I think it is appropriate to say that we only get out of life what we put into it, therefore if we do the best we can in the circumstances in which we find ourselves, we collect our prize.

Now I shall deal with other types of mate which are *not* true soulmates. I have stated earlier in this lesson that in our Destiny or Life Pattern which is mapped out for us by the Reincarnation Committee before birth and with our agreement, we are destined to have difficulties of some kind or another. These often make themselves known in the choice of marriage partner. It works like this; depending on the lesson that we have to learn and the kharmic debt that we have to pay, our marriage will be either successful, reasonable or bad.

A man and a woman are destined to meet and marry because, perhaps, one can teach the other the lesson or lessons that they need to learn. For example, a woman may be bitter, sharp-tongued, hasty-tempered and selfish, so she is paired with a loving, placid-natured, generous, softly-spoken man. The woman has to learn from the man how to control her undesirable characteristics and the man should help her to succeed. They are not aware that this is what they were brought together for, neither do they give the subject any thought, so the marriage fails. This is a kharmic case of mating but they are *not* soulmates.

The woman will have to continue to be paired with a man with similar characteristics to the one mentioned, until *she* has decided that being bitter, sharp-tongued, selfish and hasty-tempered does not get her anywhere. Realization *must* come from *within*. Not one person on this Earth is free from fault, a sweeping statement perhaps but nevertheless true. Until people look within themselves, recognize their faults and then are willing to accept guidance to correct those faults, reincarnation will have to continue and spiritual progress will be retarded.

Some people are drawn together to do a specific job of work on Earth. Pierre and Marie Curie, well known for their life's work in discovering radium salts, are two examples, among many others. They were not necessarily soulmates but each of them obviously had the essential similar characteristics in order to carry out and complete the work that has proved to be so beneficial to mankind. They had to be 'in tune' with each other.

I should now like to return to Lesson 3 and quote the case of Mr and Mrs X. You may remember that I said these two people were opposite in nature. Clearly, Mr X was destined to marry Mrs X because she could teach him a lot about life. She was responsible, loving, good-natured and kind. He was cold, aloof, unkind and shunned responsibility, although he was desirous of having all the comforts that a home and family life could provide.

Mr and Mrs X were *not* soulmates and Mr X did not learn his kharmic lessons. The result is that Mr X will have to reincarnate to learn his lessons with another woman in another life. Mrs X did her best to teach her husband what he *should* have done in life, so she will not have to be paired with a man of that type again.

In our total existence of many lives, we gain experiences of varying kinds by the kind of life that we live, through the people that we meet, the work that we choose to do and the way in which we handle our lives. All this combines to shape our characters and characteristics. We are bound to gather some bad points along with the good ones, this is inevitable. Some people have greater difficulty in shaking off their bad points than others.

Although a couple may have compatibility in many aspects of their relationship, they may not necessarily be *true* soulmates but they may both have reached the same stage of spiritual evolution, therefore they get on reasonably well. For instance, a Plane Three man would get on well with a Plane Three woman.

In the case of William Shakespeare and Ann Hathaway, their marriage stood the test of time not only because they were *true* soulmates but William needed Ann to support him in his great writing work. Ann obviously had the characteristic qualities necessary to provide that support.

The best way to complete your life with your partner is to communicate with him or her. So often lack of communication between people is the cause of marriage failure in addition to the unwillingness to confront one's faults. Co-operation between the partners is the cure for faults and this cannot be done without communication between them.

When people talk about 'looking within themselves', they are not really looking for the truth about themselves but for excuses to use for their behaviour. They do not want to know the truth or confront it because, more often than not, the truth hurts.

God does *not* dwell within us but the knowledge of our behaviour in previous lives does. The subconscious memory of that behaviour, whether good or bad, pricks the conscience so that we accept the good but reject the bad. This is falsely labelled by some as being the 'spirit of God' working within us.

Summary of Lesson 4 Part One

From this lesson we have learned the following points:
1. We do *not* pass this way once only.
2. The number of lives that we live is entirely in our own control.
3. We *must* accept the inevitable.
4. We *always* reap as we sow.
5. To resort to crime is pointless because we make a rod for our own backs.
6. If we require peace of mind, we *must* confront our faults fairly and squarely and deal with them.
7. A soulmate is a coveted prize.
8. God does NOT dwell within us.

Lesson 5   **Part One**

RESPONSIBILITY AND RIGHT THINKING

Before this world can once more be considered a reasonable place in which to live, there has to be a complete psychological rehabilitation of thought amongst its peoples.

We should *never* have to live in fear of our lives, as many of us do now, and it is a terrible indictment against present-day society that no one is safe, even in their own homes. To have to live behind locked doors and windows for most of the time is tantamount to being in prison; therefore, we have become virtual 'prisoners' of a section of irresponsible morons who have brought society to this unhappy state.

Even more terrible is the fact that some people in high places of authority have encouraged and allowed such irresponsible cretins to gain the upper hand by giving criminals sentences that were far too lenient. It is of little comfort to the victims to hear a judge say that their attacker has "suffered enough", when dispensing an inadequate sentence.

Attitudes are very important, I cannot stress this point too strongly, and it is vital to our *survival* that there is a change of attitude towards many things that affect us all, either directly or indirectly.

Whether we believe it or not, we are all spiritual beings housed in physical bodies for the duration of our stay on Earth. A *whole* person is one who has had a good academic education, a good social behaviour education and who is spiritually enlightened, which does *not* mean the acceptance of *any* religion. I shall explain.

When ethics and etiquette were observed and practised, the world was a much better place in which to live because the principles of both are *spiritual attributes*. For the benefit of those who would like some of these principles listed, here they are: politeness, courtesy, good manners, respect for oneself and for others, consideration for others, honesty, self-control, self-discipline, loyalty, trustworthiness, humility, reliability, keeping one's word, taking a pride in one's appearance and in one's work, punctuality, being self-sacrificing and living a good, clean life morally. These are just a few and, unless there is a return to such standards, today's rot will get progressively worse.

People become confused when the word 'spiritual' is mentioned. They visualize churches, kneeling in prayer, priests, choirs and congregations chanting. These are *not* spiritual attributes, they concern rituals! True spiritual attributes are all the little things that make our daily lives tolerable and which we so often ignore because they *appear* to be insignificant.

Those who have dropped their standards of ethics and etiquette in order to be 'fashionable' with the non-standards of modern times, have sinned against themselves and have not done their spiritual status any good. There is no finer training than example and those who were fortunate enough to have good standards instilled in childhood are in a wonderful position to teach the less knowledgeable. "If you can't beat 'em, join 'em," is one attitude that needs changing.

A truly spiritual person will be ethical and responsible and will listen to his or her conscience, which pricks us when we are not abiding by the rules. The number of times one attends church on Sundays or how much money one contributes to the collection box are not spiritual attributes.

The Chart supplied with this lesson shows to what degree these virtues are practised by the occupants of the different Planes in Heaven. The lower the Plane, the weaker is the virtue level. The higher the Plane, the stronger the virtue level.

However, as we are all different, it is possible that, through their own personal experiences in their existence of more than one life, a lower Plane person may have a strong conscience level but be weak in accepting responsibility, least of all for anything that they, themselves, say and do.

Plane One personnel are very unpredictable, often saying one thing but actually *doing* another. I have found, to my cost, that one of their favourite tricks is to supply wrong or misleading information. Sometimes it was deliberately done; sometimes it was owing to a total lack of awareness.

A Plane Two person can be very sound and reliable in accepting responsibility but may be weak with regard to behaving ethically, depending on *their* experiences gained during their total existence. People vary but the Chart is a good guide to spiritual attributes and awareness levels in general.

By awareness, I mean the degree to which a person is aware of that which is going on around him or her every day. It is surprising how many live in a little dream-world of their own and walk about, even in a busy street, in a state of utter unawareness. This awareness extends to a person's spiritual state too, meaning how ready and willing they are to accept spiritual knowledge from those who know and to develop their psychic abilities which are latent in all of us.

I stated in Lesson 4 that we are not all born equal, neither are we all on the same level. The Chart of Responsibility, Conscience and Ethical Levels supplied herein confirms this fact. If we were all equal and on the same level there would only be one Plane in Heaven. We determine our own level by the way in which we think and behave towards others and in our attitudes to life.

Can you imagine anyone in the Lower Astral having tea with God and observing all the niceties of etiquette? Definitely not! Low Spiritual Beings shun and run away from High Spiritual Beings. The brilliance of the aura of a High Spiritual Being blinds the Low Spiritual Being making it impossible for the one to stay in the presence of the other.

None of us can avoid responsibility of some kind or another and, with the decline in standards, comes a decline in the acceptance of responsibility. There are two main reasons for people shying away from responsibility. One is that they are afraid of becoming involved and the other is the fear of being criticized.

Owing to the adverse introduction of anarchy and libertinism, which are both side-effects of a morally soft society stemming from socialism, people have become far too aggressive, disguised as 'sensitive', over issues, so that all people who uphold law, order and good standards are considered enemies of both the State and of those who do not have any standards at all.

The people who are ethical and think rightly are abused and ridiculed by the 'no standards, no ethics, no authority' brigade who seem to win even in courts of law. This is not democracy, it is suppression of those who think rightly by those who think wrongly. Unfortunately, as the latter appeared to gain the upper hand in recent decades, it was and still is a constant battle between right and wrong.

I should now like to give some examples of attitudes in everyday situations with their resulting spiritual attributes. Some of the following reports have been taken from newspapers and news bulletins and actually happened; others are situations which have been encountered by me, personally. The right attitudes and spiritual attributes have been inserted by me.

Wrong Attitude (no spiritual attributes)
All persons of sixty years of age and over should be thrown on the scrap heap.

Right Attitude
All persons of sixty years of age and over have a wealth of experience and knowledge to offer and many make significant contributions to society. (consideration for others)

Wrong Attitude
If I need something but cannot afford to buy it, I shall steal it.

Right Attitude
Stealing is a crime. I shall save hard to buy the article I need, then I shall appreciate it all the more.
(honesty)

Wrong Attitude (no spiritual attributes)
I only go to work each day for the money. I don't care about

my job, my employer or the customers.

Right Attitude
If I work willingly, show an interest in the products of my firm and am pleasant to the customers, I could get promotion or even *own* the business one day.
(loyalty)

Wrong Attitude
Joe Bloggs is convicted of murder and is sentenced to life imprisonment. The misguided community campaign for his release.

Right Attitude
Joe Bloggs has had a fair trial and been found guilty. He must pay the price demanded of him. Let justice be done.
(correct judgement)

Wrong Attitude
A seventeen-year-old commits murder, is convicted and sentenced. Social workers play on emotion, "He didn't ask to be born into this society" etc. Society clubs together to buy him a house!
(This actually happened)

Right Attitude
No matter what age the murderer is, he or she must pay for the crime, *not* be encouraged to do it again upon release from prison because of misplaced sympathy.
(correct judgement)

Wrong Attitude
A disinterested shop assistant throws an item in front of a customer without a word. The attitude is, "Take it or leave it, mate!"

Right Attitude
Allowing for *very* trying customers, the assistant should greet the new customer pleasantly and with a smile. After all, the new customer is not responsible for the last one's rudeness.
(politeness and courtesy)

Wrong Attitude
I'm going to play my stereo as loudly as I like even though it is 2.00 a.m. and everyone is asleep.

Right Attitude
When I play my stereo, presently, I shall put my headphones on so that I will not disturb the neighbours.
(concern for others)

Wrong Attitude
What right has anyone else to tell *me* what to do!

Right Attitude
If no one corrects me I shall never know right from wrong. I should be grateful that people take sufficient interest in me to ensure that I stay out of trouble and harm.
(humility)

Wrong Attitude (no spiritual attributes)
The police are my enemies. They try to stop me from behaving as *I* want to.

Right Attitude
The police have a very difficult job to do. They protect *me* from the crimes of others. Without them there would be unacceptable lawlessness to which *I* might fall victim. I shall support them and report any crimes that I witness. Conversely, if I am belligerent, I must expect them to retaliate.
(trustworthiness and loyalty)

Wrong Attitude
A man is convicted of a savage rape attack. The judge allows him to go free just because the rapist happens to come from the same town as the judge.
(another actual incident)

Right Attitude
This is not justice, it is pure bias. The judge should have considered the feelings of the victim and passed a deterrent sentence on the man. Rape is an inexcusable act of terrorism and should be suitably punished.
(concern for others)

Wrong Attitude
"Of course, *nobody* knows the answer to...." (whatever it is)

Right Attitude
It is wrong to say that *nobody* knows the answer to anything because *somebody, somewhere,* might have the answer and the key to many philosophical questions but they are sitting on them for fear of being ridiculed. Often the truth is much stranger and different from widely-held beliefs.
(humility)

Wrong Attitude
There is nobody watching me so I won't bother to do my job properly. I'll just skip through it.

Right Attitude
If you are going to do a job at all, do it well and properly. When you *think* nobody is looking, somebody usually is! Shoddy work can cost lives.
(reliability and trustworthiness)

When discipline ruled, life was better because a disciplined person is a happy, reliable person. When authority was respected, life was less stressful and easier to live because in a well-balanced society *we* have both discipline and respectful conformity with legally constituted authority. Both of these virtues are high spiritual attributes.

Those who decided to rebel against the old system of ethics, etiquette, morals, discipline and authority that was extant in the early part of the twentieth century, are now reaping as they have sowed. Teachers are unable to cope with unruly, undisciplined pupils. Crime has increased to such an alarming extent that the police force are stretched to capacity to contain it. An amoral permissiveness has led to the rapid spread of AIDS, anarchy and libertinism.

Selfishness is prevalent, standards hardly exist and even professional people have not escaped being tainted by the brush of militant foolhardiness. The very people who ought to be setting an example are not doing so because they are often making money out of hostile situations.

Misplaced sympathy abounds, so that the criminal is admired and the poor victim is ignored. Responsibility is not accepted any more and people will go out of their way to shift it on to someone else's shoulders.

Unchecked, all this can only, eventually, lead to one thing — total collapse of a civilization. In short, Sodom and Gomorrah again or the Roman Empire.

In allowing misguided, misapplied socialism into places of importance and into our thoughts and attitudes, we have lost our spirituality. I can only say that our Creator must look upon the inhabitants of the world He created with a great sadness, perhaps pity. Our only hope is to return to the days of gentleness, courtesy and good manners. It *can* be done!

Summary of Lesson 5 Part One

From this lesson we have learned the following:
1. That most of us need to change our attitudes regarding many things of vital importance.
2. That true spiritual attributes lie in the practice of altruistic behaviour and right thinking.

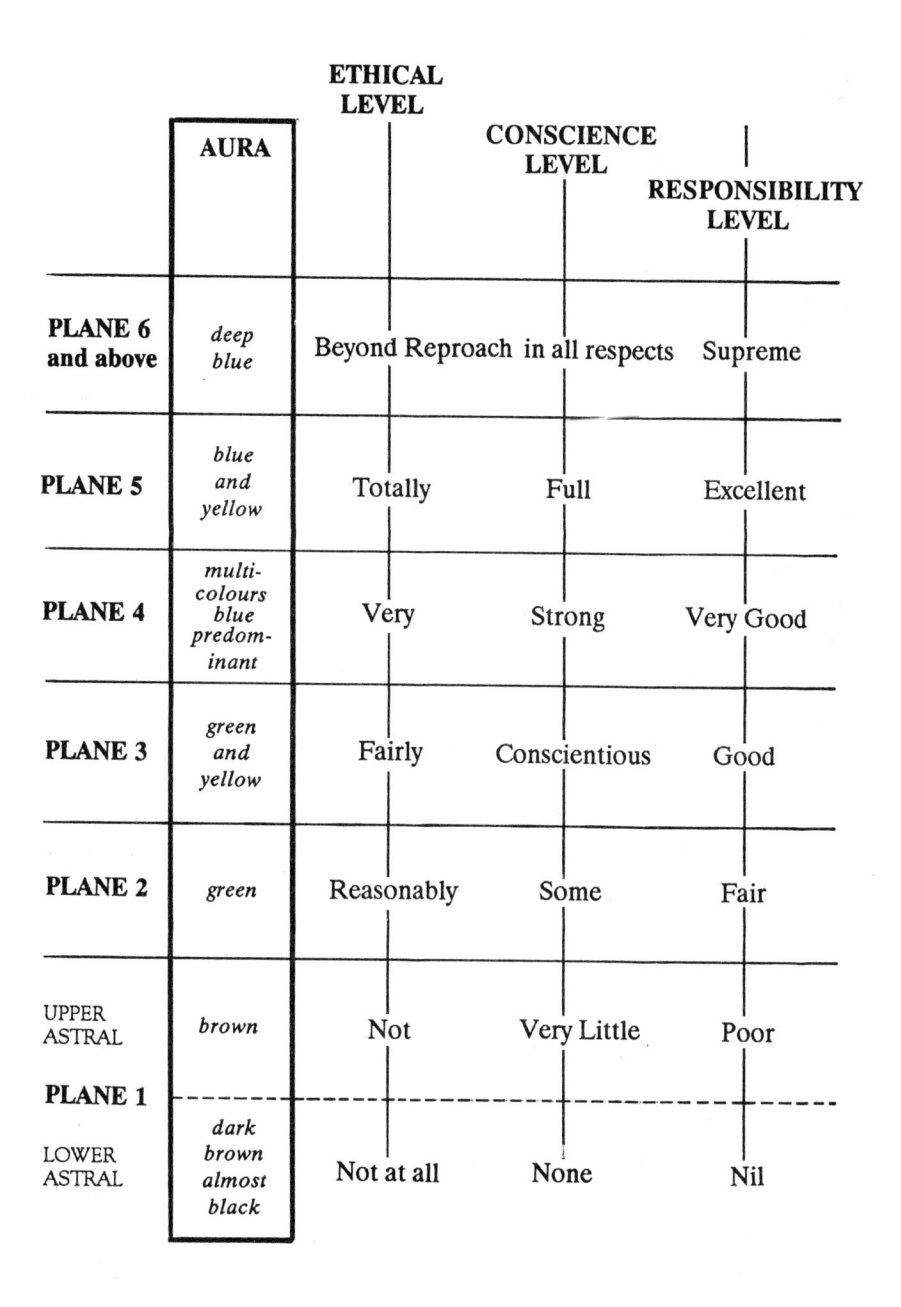

	AURA	ETHICAL LEVEL	CONSCIENCE LEVEL	RESPONSIBILITY LEVEL
PLANE 6 and above	deep blue	Beyond Reproach in all respects		Supreme
PLANE 5	blue and yellow	Totally	Full	Excellent
PLANE 4	multicolours blue predominant	Very	Strong	Very Good
PLANE 3	green and yellow	Fairly	Conscientious	Good
PLANE 2	green	Reasonably	Some	Fair
UPPER ASTRAL PLANE 1	brown	Not	Very Little	Poor
LOWER ASTRAL	dark brown almost black	Not at all	None	Nil

The Chart of Responsibility, Conscience and Ethical Levels

Lesson 6 **Part One**

THE MIND

In writing this lesson, I have been greatly helped by Professor Doctor Carl Gustav Jung, the eminent Swiss psychologist and psychiatrist, who was born in 1875 and died in 1961.

In order to produce the quality of communication peculiar to Professor Jung and to do his work justice, it was necessary to have a remarkable affinity with him and to have a fair understanding of his work. I am honoured to say that I do have a deep affinity with him and the following scripts on the Mind and Insidious-type Psychopaths, are the result of my many consultations with him on these two subjects.

The Mind is a spiritual entity and is not physical. It cannot be taken and examined under a microscope. This is where scientists, psychologists and psychiatrists become confused because, as the brain is the computer of the physical body and is responsible for its locomotion, so the Mind is the computer of the spiritual body and is the centre of our whole being.

Few people *really* understand the Mind or how it works therefore, for the purposes of explanation, I shall divide the Mind into four parts. Part one of the Mind is hasty, reactive and sometimes hostile. Part two of the Mind is rational and logical and analyses available data. Part three of the Mind is psychosomatic. Part four of the Mind is the subconscious.

The Mind Part One
   Unfortunately, it is all too common for people to bring this part of their minds into play spontaneously instead of using their rational, analytical minds. This causes so much trouble. Many mountains have been made out of molehills because of the reaction of part one of the Mind which can be a fearful, deadly weapon.

Let us take a hypothetical example. Mr Brown is the manager of a firm of builders and decorators known as Messrs. White & Sons who employ several people. One of the employees, called Thomas, is constantly late for work and has a reputation for idleness. When he *does* do any work, it is substandard. He is rude to potential customers and is a known trouble-maker.

Mr Brown has good reason to give Thomas a ticking-off and proceeds to do this in his office. Thomas, knowing that he is guilty of the charges, denies behaving in that manner because part one of the Mind harbours resentment and reacts as soon as it is attacked. Considerations of right and wrong do not enter the Reactive Mind. The mere fact that it is being attacked is enough to set alarm bells ringing inside it and the defences are up immediately. In trying to save his face under the barrage of criticism and accusation, Thomas clutches at flying straws in a desperate attempt to avoid admonishment of any kind. He looks for a scapegoat; the system is wrong, the customers are too particular, his workmates are difficult to get along with, the work is too hard, the hours are too long, the other person did not do their job correctly which affected his work. The tale of woe continues.

In no time at all, Mr Brown has a strike on his hands and becomes the unwitting target of bitterness from the remainder of his staff. Hostility in their Reactive Minds has been stimulated by Thomas who lost no time in getting misplaced sympathy from the others in order to strengthen his position on the battlefield.

Thomas is unwilling to admit responsibility for his guilt because to do this would be demeaning to the image that he has built up for himself.

In cases like this one, it is very important to the person who began the fracas that their image should remain intact and they will fight tooth and nail to preserve it. The hasty, reactive, hostile part of the Mind plays too prominent a role in daily life and this manifests itself in many ways.

When some people are confronted with their behavioural patterns, familiar signs appear such as fidgeting, mind-wandering, fake loss of memory, evading the questions asked and twisting facts so that they appear to the *advantage* of the offender instead of to the *disadvantage*. Always there is a shift of responsibility on to the other person.

How many times have any of us wished that we had not said or done a certain thing? How many times have any of us wished that we had *thought* more about what we had said and done *before* speaking or taking action? How many times have any of us realized, *after the event*, that things would have been better if we had analysed the situation before reacting so hastily?

It is easy to *say* that we should not react hastily but not as easy to *do* it. However, if a determined effort is made, using plenty of self-control, to keep part one of our Minds under subjection, then we are half-way to avoiding unpleasantries. As in all things, practice makes perfect.

The Mind Part Two

This is the sensible part of the Mind. The logical, rational, analytical part that checks us when we are tempted to be too hasty and reactive but, unfortunately, it is often ignored with disastrous results.

Listening a lot more to part two of our Minds will tell us to stop, look and listen before crossing the busy road of anger, bitterness, provocation and incitement. It will tell us to take time to consider a situation before making any decisions. It will tell us to reason things out before committing ourselves to a series of regrets.

The application of pure common sense which comes from the logical, rational, analytical part of our Minds ensures that errors of judgement are less likely to occur and there should be a reduction in aberrations.

If Thomas, mentioned earlier, had faced facts about himself and owned up to the charges levelled against him, the strike would have been avoided, there would have been no disruption of work and the manager's job would have been much easier.

Obviously, the best method of confronting our faults is not to have any! However, Thomas bitterly resented being told some truths about himself, so he caused a lot more trouble to try to justify himself. If Thomas had used his part two Mind instead of his part one Mind, he would have apologized for his behaviour and then taken the consequences, for the sake of the firm and the other employees. The modern concept that it is a sign of weakness to apologize to anybody for anything is wrong. It is a false concept born of false pride which always heralds a fall.

The Mind Part Three
This is the section of our Minds that cossets and shields us from our enemies. How many of us have suffered toothache until we can no longer bear it then, after making an appointment with the dentist or arriving on his doorstep, it disappears? How many of us have worked ourselves into a state of nerves before taking an important examination because we have already convinced ourselves that we shall fail it? On the day of the examination the psychosomatic part of our Mind says, "We shall have a thumping headache today!" The examination is missed but, shortly after it is known to be over, the headache vanishes and the subject feels better!

It is truly amazing how the Mind can affect us either for good or for bad. When we are keen on doing something that interests us, the Mind can be a wonderful stimulant spurring us on with tremendous enthusiasm. When we have to do something unpleasant, the Mind will play to our mood and the self-pity pours forth, deliberately exacerbating the situation.

This is very common among all age groups and is not confined to any particular type of person. Self-pity is manipulated to gain sympathy from others who can be put to a lot of unnecessary trouble, expense and even worry on behalf of the sufferer, only to discover, later, that the original problem was not as bad as the sufferer had painted it.

How we handle our Mind when it starts operating adversely is our responsibility. We *can* manage our lives successfully if we are aware of the tricks that the Mind can play upon us in given situations and if we are in possession of knowledge concerning the existence of those tricks.

The Mind Part Four

This is the Subconscious part of our Minds. Memory is spiritual. It is *not* the result of activity by brain cells or any other cellular action. The Mind stores memories not only of our present lives but of events that have happened to us in all our spiritual existence of several lives. The latter are stored in the subconscious which has already been explained in earlier lessons. The Mind is, in fact, a miniature, personal Akashic Record. It motivates us and is the centre of intelligence, however sharp or dull.

Emotion is triggered by the Psychosomatic part of our Minds and this can be either genuine or aberrated, misplaced emotion. Events stored in the Subconscious part of our Minds may be re-stimulated by almost any present-time incident, a word, a tone of voice, a picture, a place, an artefact of some kind.

The logical part of the Mind will take the re-stimulated information that has come from the Subconscious and use it to advantage. The Reactive part of the Mind takes the information from the Subconscious and uses it to make the person feel ill, aided and abetted by sympathy from the Psychosomatic part of the Mind.

The Insidious-type Psychopath
Definition of words:

insidious = watching an opportunity to ensnare, intended to entrap, deceptive.

psychopath = one who shows a degree of emotional instability without mental disorder.

The following script concerns an increasing number of people in present-day society. It is designed to try to help those who are in close proximity to this type of person and to try to help them to understand the position in which they find themselves. I shall refer to the person or persons closest to the insidious-type psychopath as 'the victim' or 'the victims' because that is exactly what they are.

The insidious-type psychopath can be either male or female and may be found in any walk of life. They are not normally categorized as mentally ill but they live under a compulsive and continual urge to make their presence felt regardless of any other consideration.

They can be clever, intelligent and educated or the opposite of these. Typical characteristics are: covert jealousy, selfishness, possessiveness, exaggeration, self-pity — the 'nobody understands me' syndrome — dislike of quietness and a deep resentment of anyone who is closely associated with them and who happens to be in the limelight for some reason.

If the psychopath considers that a person is inferior to him in knowledge, ability and education, then he expresses anger and impatience until he has managed to focus everyone's attention on to himself.

Self-indulgence is apparent, in that personal pleasures *must* come *first* before any work or study. Work, study or both, are serious interruptions to a psychopath's programme and both are deeply resented. The wishes of the victim or other relatives and friends are either completely disregarded or treated as being of secondary consideration.

Personal possessions are of prime concern and importance to a psychopath. These can be inanimate objects or, worse still, a person. When applied to objects, the psychopath will constantly remind his listener of "*my* car/house/garden/piano/stereo/records" and so on. If animals are involved then it is "*my* cat/dog/bird/horse" and so on, with the emphasis always heavily put on the word '*my*'. No mention is made of the psychopath's husband or wife having any part in the possession.

If a person is involved, then that person is to be pitied because he or she does not get much of a life, hence the term 'victim'. Every movement is watched by the psychopath, every word is monitored and, at times, it would seem that even every *thought* of the victim is monitored. Covert jealousy of the victim's freedom is high-lighted and often unfounded, therefore the victims of the insidious-type psychopath are likely to become devious themselves in order to safeguard *their* sanity.

The insidious-type psychopath has a suspicious mind and often a vivid imagination also, and will mentally create adverse situations where, in fact, none exists. For example, if a group of people are talking and laughing amongst themselves, the psychopath, watching from a short distance, immediately suspects that he or she is the subject of their frivolous discussion.

The psychopath's Reactive Mind goes to work and invents all sorts of ridiculous accusations upon which he or she will dwell. Inevitably, at a suitable opportunity, the victim is at the receiving end of the psychopath's mistrust.

This is bound to affect the behaviour of the victim and others, in close proximity to the psychopath, who may become unwitting targets. They all react in ways which are alien to their better natures in order to survive life with the psychopath who is extremely difficult and almost impossible with whom to live.

The insidious-type psychopath loves to exaggerate and complicate situations deliberately for effect, especially if it concerns themselves. This can often be very embarrassing for the victim because the victim can be involved as well. Any compromising situation thoroughly delights the psychopath who secretly chuckles at the discomfort felt by the victim.

However, should the tables turn and things go wrong, the psychopath will blame everything and everybody except himself. In any attempted confrontation of their behaviour, the psychopath will vehemently deny that his conduct is abnormal and is most emphatic that the reason for other people thinking that he is aberrated is pure imagination on their part. 'People don't understand me', is the plea.

It is useless to argue with the insidious-type psychopath because having stated that they have no faults, confrontation is impossible. In the advanced stages of this kind of psychosis the psychopath is convinced of his or her perfection.

Another predominant trait of the insidious-type psychopath is that of argumentativeness. The psychopath yearns for attention and will seize any opportunity to start an argument, very often over a triviality. Once again, the long-suffering victim is the target who responds in a manner which is distasteful to them. The victim, becoming exasperated by the repeated attacks on their reason might well tell the psychopath a few home truths! Immediately, the psychopath, never one to miss a trick, will retaliate by twisting the home truths to his advantage.

Later, aware that he has caused an unnecessary scene, he will propitiate with a gift of some kind or a gentle gesture of kindness.

The insidious-type psychopath will give 'tit for tat' as found in young children at play, "You didn't offer me one of your sweeties, so I shan't offer you any of mine," type of thing. In any conversation with the victim, the psychopath delights in talking to, and treating, the victim as though he or she were a child.

The insidious-type psychopath will deliberately tout for trouble; for example, when speed is called for because of a forthcoming engagement and time is running short, he will put a 'go slow' policy into operation. Knowing that sooner or later those who are waiting are bound to try to hurry him, the psychopath will reduce every movement to a snail's pace just to annoy, aggravate, hinder and upset everyone concerned. The gilt has been taken off the gingerbread before any enjoyment can be anticipated.

The insidious-type psychopath secretly gloats over the fact that he has caused disruption and anger because this gives him a secure feeling of power and domination over his victims. He will constantly complain about the noise other people make but thinks nothing of creating a dreadful disturbance when other people wish to be quiet. The fox is renowned for its cunning and the psychopath can be compared with the crafty fox.

The insidious-type psychopath is easily re-stimulated by influences around him and will slip into an engrammic state immediately. The Subconscious Mind in a psychopath is highly vulnerable and acute to stimulus. The re-stimulant can take the form of almost anything, a word harshly spoken, a gesture, a landscape scene or an inanimate object.

Psychiatrists, not fully understanding the structure of the engram, will pump the patient full of drugs, when all that is needed is a very competent counsellor. Drugs only add to the patient's confusion and misery and further bewilder the helpless relatives.

The victims of an insidious-type psychopath need to have the stamina of an ox if they are to survive living with such a person. However, little hope can be held out to them except that they be given as much knowledge and understanding of the situation as possible.

An insidious-type psychopath will not change because he sees no need for change, therefore he is best left on his own to care for himself. If this is not possible because of infirmity of some kind, then the victims have no choice but to try to understand the situation that they are in, with help from the information contained in this script.

I hope that by now a good picture has been given of how the Mind works on our behalf either to our advantage or to our disadvantage. *Less* emphasis on part one of the Mind, the Reactive and much *more* emphasis on part two of the Mind, the logical analytical, sensible part, is essential if we are to avoid misunderstandings and unpleasantness in daily life.

It is difficult but not impossible for some people to put aside deep-rooted opinions and ideas, especially those concerning religious subjects. Very few who have returned to Heaven still hold the same views as they did when incarnate, after their re-education in Heaven. Even erudite professors have had to abandon their preconceptions and to re-learn many philosophical concepts, which surprised them!

It is essential to our spiritual progress that we have some idea of how the Mind works because then we can be ready to handle the pitfalls that suddenly appear before us. In this lesson, with Professor Jung's help, I hope I have clarified some aspects of the working of The Mind.

Summary of Lesson 6 Part One

In this lesson we have learned the following:
1. That we must be cautious of the Reactive Part of our Minds, part one, that causes most of the trouble in daily life and we must try to keep it under control.
2. That we must encourage the use of part two of our Minds, the sensible, logical, rational, analytical part which is so often ignored in times of stress. This part of the Mind is the 'early warning' system that tells us to stop, look and listen.
3. That we must beware of the Psychosomatic Part of our Minds, part three, that fills us with misguided sympathy and self-pity when we are unwilling to confront a problem.
4. That if we are unfortunate enough to be the victim of an insidious-type psychopath, we must try to be brave, patient and understanding. Pray that you may be given strength to bear your cross. This is all you can do.

Lesson 7   **Part One**

COMMUNICATION COMPREHENSION

Communication comprehension or understanding communication between people appears to be a lost art. It requires more skill than people realize, in order to avoid unfavourable complications. Frequently, whatever is said is either misconstrued, twisted to mean something quite different from that which the speaker intended or is taken by listeners as a personal slight, attack, invalidation or criticism of them.

How many of us *really listen* when someone is speaking? If they are talking about an interesting subject or something which personally involves the listener, then concentration is not difficult. On the other hand, if the conversation does not interest the listener or is not what the listener *wants* to hear, then the attention wanders and an excuse is found to depart.

The most common causes of breakdowns in relationships between people are insufficient and inefficient communication. Other reasons are a lack of knowledge and understanding of a given situation; the inability to express oneself fully and properly; a poor education; disinterest in people or events or both and the withholding of information either because of mistrust of the other person or the deliberate intention to mislead that person.

The theme of modern society is to find an excuse for personal behaviour at all costs. What can we do about it? The answer is, take time to listen and do not be in so much of a hurry. If the pace of living were slowed down considerably, there would not be so many misunderstandings in communication between people.

We cannot avoid communication with others, be they human or animals. If one has a pet dog or cat then, first thing in the morning, the animal will wake its owner for attention. The cat purrs and cries until it is let out. The dog fetches its lead to prompt its owner that exercise time has arrived! It is their **way** of communicating. A baby will cry when it needs attention because it cannot yet speak. Neither humans nor the animal or insect world can exist without some form of communication with one another.

People's attitudes while communicating are all-important. The tone of voice used and the way words are spoken can either make or mar communication. Failure to understand another's vocabulary is a communication block. It is a good idea to remember or write down any word used that is unfamiliar and then look it up in a dictionary at the first opportunity.

Many people misunderstand because the vocabulary used is beyond their comprehension. Some are too proud to ask for an explanation and will not be bothered to search a dictionary, therefore meaning goes right over their heads which leads to complete confusion and misunderstanding of the subject. Learning is a continuing process and stretches across the whole of existence, consisting of our present lives, our previous ones and our retraining in Heaven between incarnations.

Before commencing communication with people in Heaven, many need to learn how to communicate with those around them on Earth first! Good communication with people in Heaven can become well-established if you are a good communicant with those around you in daily life. Here, one may be tempted to exclaim, "Oh, but I *am* a very good conversationalist!" Yes, so one may be but how good a *listener* are you? The art of good communication needs good listeners as well as good talkers.

Here is an explanation of some types of communication and an example of the Communication Cycle.

The Communication Cycle

Bill   *Tom*
sends   receives but gives no reply

RESULT = Bill's confusion, loss of interest, perhaps even anger.

Correct communication
sends   receives and acknowledges

RESULT = cycle of communication has been completed. Bill is satisfied.

Communication breakdowns
sends   receives but has mental barriers owing to aberrated attitudes. Gives aberrated, emotive reply

RESULT = Bill is confused because communication has failed.

Communication is a means of conveying meaning, intention, ideas or data from one mind to another.
    Types of communication are:

(a) Speech   (b) Visual   (c) Touch
(d) Audio   (e) Telepathic   (f) Writing
(g) Reading   (h) Music   (i) Signalling
(j) Shaking hands (k) Baby crying   (l) Animal sounds
(m) Telephone   (n) Instinctive (auric and psychic)
(o) Violence (aberrated communication)

There are many more kinds of communication of course but it is not possible to list them all.
    Further misunderstandings in communication are largely owing to garbled speech, a half-hearted attempt to explain the

point in question, insufficient knowledge of the subject under discussion, a noisy background making hearing very difficult and, in some cases, a deliberate desire to mislead the listener. The latter could be because the speaker feels guilty over some misdemeanour and wishes to cover up his behaviour.

Consideration for one another in conversation is desirable and is a point of Ethics. For instance, if one person is deaf, the other person should not attempt to hold a conversation with the afflicted one in a noisy environment but suggest that they move to a quieter place.

When speaking to an elderly person whose faculties are not as sharp as they used to be but who is none the less still very intelligent, avoid talking to them as though they were simple, for this can be very annoying and, even insulting, to a Senior Citizen and will quickly create a communication breakdown.

Children are often more understanding and intelligent than they are given credit for. Avoid using words that are beyond their vocabulary but explain any word used which has not been understood. A little extra time and patience spent on explaining things to young, enquiring minds, pays dividends in the long run.

A good conversationalist does not try to monopolize a conversation but will observe that others wish to contribute and will grant them the opportunity to do so.

The principles needed for good communication between incarnate people also apply to communication with discarnate people. All people, whether incarnate or discarnate are living, moving, feeling, thinking beings. When communicating with discarnate people one is not talking to wisps of thin air or diaphanous phantoms!

One's approach to communication with someone in the next world should be friendly, sincere and genuine. Genuine in as much as one is seeking knowledge irrespective of that which one already *thinks* one knows. This is one pitfall that besets many beginners in this specialized type of communication. The incarnate communicant's attitude to the heavenly communicant, if dictatorial or full of disbelief, will easily discourage him or her just as an incarnate person would be discouraged if treated like that. Hostility is quickly sensed by the heavenly communicant, spoiling any chance of establishing communication.

Treat your discarnate friend as an intelligent being who is in possession of more details than you are, no matter how many years of study lie behind you. Have no fear of the discarnate person. Fear is a common communication block and can prevent communication from even starting, no matter how keen the incarnate person is to establish rapport.

This fear is capable of being deep in the subconscious mind, a hangover from a previous life incident, but the incarnate communicant is not even aware of its existence. It can also be a very real, very aware incident in the incarnate communicant's present life over which they are afraid their spiritual communicant might take them to task.

When one is in communication with a spiritual person, one must be prepared to be told things about oneself, however delicately they are put, and this is where a lot of would-be communicants fail because they cannot bear to be 'told off' if the occasion warrants it. What is done is done, and one cannot turn the clock back. One must proceed. Therefore, face up to whatever you did and then try to make amends or enquire how you might do this.

The best methods of communicating with the other world are either by using a ouija board or by writing. We will take the ouija board first. Everyone is familiar with its lay-out so I will not take time to explain it. One needs absolute quiet and must be assured of having no interruptions. Have paper and pen or pencil beside you to write down that which is received. Be relaxed, have patience and wait; maybe these requisites are hard for you to develop but persevere!

The spiritual being, seeing that you are genuinely waiting to hear what he has to say, will think of a word and then spell it out using his mind and energy to move your arm around the ouija board. Inter-world communication is not easy at first. It is tiring for both sides therefore do not go beyond fifteen minutes to start with, gradually increasing the time as efficiency is acquired.

Have courage and do not be afraid of the spiritual energy which is pouring through your arm. You may change arms at any time, asking your spiritual communicant to wait while you do so. Speak either by telepathy or by using your natural voice, it makes no difference. You may ask your spiritual communicant to wait while you write down that which comes through. Date all communications and log the time started and the time finished.

At first, odd letters will be given to you that make no sense at all. Be patient, this is your psychic channel opening. Gradually, short words should be received, then longer ones, then sentences, all of which should make sensible reading. By the time you are receiving sentences, you should be getting a whole, complete sentence by just receiving the initial letter. For example, the sentence, "How are you today?" should have been picked up by the incarnate communicant at the receipt of the letter 'H'.

Constant daily practice is the only answer to attaining perfect communication with your spiritual communicant. *Always* get your communicant's name. Never communicate with anyone who does not give a name. *You* are in charge of the whole proceedings and may finish them at any time. Where many people fail in using the ouija board or the writing method is that they do not know how to sift the information that they receive.

Naturally, because one is in touch with someone in a different dimension, there are bound to be discrepancies. The secret is knowing how to work out these discrepancies by using a good question-and-answer routine until they have all been ironed out.

Never take anything too literally but work at it until you are both satisfied that the information you have been given is correct. It is quite common for emotion to be experienced during sessions. The spiritual communicant *knows* what you are about to think and say and, as your psychic ability and awareness develop, you will pick up what is in the mind of your spiritual friend.

This is good, it means that a good rapport has been established between you and your spiritual friend who, by helping and advising *you,* enhances his or her own spiritual status in Heaven. This makes good, two-way communication between the two worlds a very important issue.

The writing method is conducted on much the same lines as the ouija board, only pen and paper are substituted for the glass and letters. The spiritual communicant takes control of your writing arm and, using his mind and energy, writes through you.

Spirit writing, *not* automatic writing, because it is not automatic, someone has to use mind, thoughts and intelligence to write, should be written sensibly and *not* with all words joined. It can be received at a very fast pace which the incarnate communicant will find hard to keep up with. Ask your spiritual friend to slow down and they will. The fast pace is owing to the difference in the 'time apparency' between the two worlds.

Now to come to those who seem to get nowhere, no matter how hard they try. There *must* be a reason for the non-starters and, in all probability, the reason lies within themselves either subconsciously or consciously. Perhaps it is jealousy, fear of admonishment or dislike of confrontation. Maybe the incarnate would-be communicant has a superiority complex, the "I know better than you" familiar pattern. All these can be present-time problems or they can be subliminal.

I said right in the beginning that attitudes were of vital importance and the only thing for the non-starters is for them to examine their own attitudes, very closely indeed. After doing this quite fairly, the non-starters need to listen most carefully to any criticism of faults of theirs that they may have without bearing resentment or malice.

In most, if not all, cases, changes of attitudes towards vital points are both necessary and essential before one can get anywhere at all with communication.

Truth is stranger than fiction and this applies to the teaching of spiritual matters too, for the world has had almost two thousand years of wrong religious teaching. I hope to put this wrong, right, in my Course.

Summary of Lesson 7 Part One

In this lesson we have learned the following:
1. That communication is vital and is an art to be worked at.
2. That not many people fully understand how to communicate skilfully.
3. That good, unaberrated communication demands more skill than is realized.
4. That the abilities of patience, being a good listener and sifting information in order to get it right, are essential.
5. That our own attitudes in communicating with those in both worlds should be given top priority.

Lesson 8 — Part One

THE HARMONY AND DISCORD SCALE

The Harmony and Discord Scale indicates the range of emotional conditions that every human being is capable of experiencing. At some point in our daily lives, we all experience one or the other of the feelings listed below. Unless stuck in a very low level on the Scale, people slide up and down the Harmony and Discord Scale several times a day.

Harmony (desirable)
Elation
Happiness
Cheerfulness
Enthusiasm
Strong interest
Positivity
Courage
Well-being
Full health
Peace of mind
Contentment
Success
Concern for others
Winning
Merit
Extroversion
Being honourable
Having sympathy

Discord (undesirable)
Indifference
Misery
Grief
Negativity
Disinterest
Fear
Sickness
Resentment
Discontentment
Anxiety
Boredom
Anger
Failure
Hatred
Self-neglect
Losing
Being dishonourable
Discredit
Introversion
Hostility
Despair
Apathy

One moment we can be enjoying wonderful happiness, then news comes to make us sad or put us in a state of grief. We can be feeling very pleased with ourselves over a successful business deal, then hear that we have lost all our money on the Stock Exchange.

We can feel very positive and enthusiastic in starting a project which demands a certain amount of courage to do it then, when it comes to seeing it through, negativity and the fear of failure creep in. Peace of mind can be shattered in seconds by a telephone call informing us of an accident that has happened to a person whom we know. We can be full of well-being for our fellow men, then be caught up in a strike that prevents us from proceeding with holiday arrangements.

All sorts of conditions can occur to alter one's position on the Scale, in a matter of minutes, causing rapid changes of emotion. There is also a permanent level that indicates the general long-term state of mind of the individual. I am sure that at some time we have all met the hypochondriac, the angry one, the lugubrious person and the cheerful one.

We can be strongly interested in our job of work, then the manager decides to promote a junior. Knowing that the promotion should have been ours, strong interest quickly turns to disinterest, discontent, bitterness, anger and hostility. The undesirable traits outnumber the desirable ones. The feelings that are listed on the Scale can be lingering or momentary depending on the situation.

The first six emotional conditions, listed on the Harmony side of the Scale, are short-lived with many people but all of these emotional conditions can be assumed rapidly for social occasions, otherwise people are on a lower, permanent level on the Scale.

For instance, most of us have brightened up considerably upon meeting someone unexpectedly in the street, or expressed delight upon answering the door-bell to find a beloved relative or friend. It can work in reverse, of course, and we could be sent into a state of fear or anxiety, when caught in these situations.

Encounters with those whom we do not desire to meet can cause any one of the undesirable emotions listed on the Discord side of the Scale. They can even cause temporary illness! This kind of short-term variation on the Scale is very common. Immediately one's spirits fall, a rapid descent on the Harmony and Discord Scale ensues.

To understand how our emotions work is advantageous because it improves our understanding of existence both in the physical and the spiritual worlds. The higher one is on the spiritual scale, as shown in Lesson 2, the better one is capable of controlling one's emotions.

Knowing how the Mind works, as set out in Lesson 6, is extremely beneficial. The combination of the tuition given in Lesson 6 and this lesson should give every student of the Course a far greater understanding of themselves.

To know that every human emotion there is can be manipulated by one or the other of the four parts of one's Mind, is a mighty weapon that can be used for good or for evil; *we* have the choice. This is why there is always a constant struggle between good and evil in this world.

The Reactive Part of the Mind takes over because it is so easily available. The Analytical Part of the Mind requires effort to think a situation out clearly and logically, which many people are reluctant to do.

The following points to remember are a good guide in everyday life:

(1) Always accept responsibility for your own condition on the Harmony and Discord Scale.
(2) Believe strongly that *you* can improve it.
(3) Do not hesitate to seek qualified help from an experienced, trustworthy person.
(4) Understand that if you find yourself near the bottom of the Scale, you are in even greater need of assistance from others.
(5) The lower one is on the Scale, the more difficult it is to raise oneself.
(6) Movement up or down on the Discord side of the Scale is

normally fairly slow.
(7) Movement up or down on the Harmony side of the Scale can often be quite rapid.

Knowledge of the Harmony and Discord Scale and the way in which people can move on it, is an invaluable aid to communication. One will find that if one is near the top of the Harmony Scale, communication with someone near the bottom of the Discord Scale will be extremely difficult if not impossible. In order to communicate with such people one has to begin by talking to them at a level which they can accept.

One's permanent state on the Scale, e.g. Cheerful, Happy, Interested, Indifferent, Miserable, Negative or Resentful, is related to one's spiritual height, in general.

An incarnate person who is fairly well up the spiritual scale, say Plane Three or Plane Four spiritual height, can be driven down to the level of Failure, Self-neglect or Losing on the Discord Scale through illness, accident or external influences such as living with a suppressive person. Normally, anyone of this spiritual height who finds themselves in the adverse circumstances mentioned, will handle their difficulties very well and recuperate from trauma fairly quickly.

An incarnate person further down the spiritual scale, say Plane One, for example, will not handle similar adverse circumstances very well. The Part One Mind of that person, the Reactive Part, exacerbates the situation and causes further resentment, anger and perhaps hatred.

Lessons 6, 7 and 8 are closely connected with spiritual height, spiritual progress and spiritual understanding. Life is a very complicated business indeed but a thorough study of the first part of this Course should have prepared students well for the second part.

It is recommended that frequent reference be made to all the lessons in Part One of the Course, especially if one encounters any of the situations that have been mentioned and covered in Part One. Try to discover *your* permanent level on the Harmony and Discord Scale.

Summary of Lesson 8 Part One

In this lesson we have learned the following:
1. We have many emotional experiences daily.
2. The higher we are spiritually, the better we can cope with life, people and communication.
3. The lower we are spiritually, the less we are able to cope with life, people and communication.
4. Our demeanour to others is more important than we realize.

END OF PART ONE OF THE COURSE.

Lesson 9   **Part Two**

THE KINGDOM OF HEAVEN

Part Two of the Course begins with a description of Plane Six which is the *real* Kingdom of Heaven. People have been led to believe, by their religious leaders, that the 'Kingdom of Heaven' is reached immediately upon passing into the next world but this is not true. Plane Six is the highest point in Heaven that anyone can attain. Beyond Plane Six lies the domain of the Spiritual Hierarchy which I shall be explaining in further lessons.

Plane Six, the Kingdom of Heaven, is a magnificent place containing equally magnificent spiritual beings. It is open to everyone, not only to those who achieved fame when incarnate. Well-known Greek thinkers and academics such as Aristotle, Plato, Hippocrates, Socrates, and Pythagoras dwell there, together with famous personalities such as Leonardo da Vinci, Michelangelo, Thomas Edison, William Shakespeare, Ann Hathaway, Florence Nightingale, Beethoven, Mozart, Dr Albert Schweitzer, Sir Isaac Newton, Sir Malcolm Campbell, and Professor Dr Carl Gustav Jung who helped me to write Lesson 6 in Part One of this Course.

Plane Six is, of course, inhabited by many, many other spiritual beings who, when they were incarnate, benefited mankind greatly by the work that they did and were equally famous in their respective disciplines. I have given only a few names in order to show the type of person who reaches such exalted heights. Entry to the Kingdom of Heaven, as shown on the full Chart of Spiritual Existence given with this lesson, is by merit after several incarnations of hardships and difficulties.

Every adversity that we have had to endure throughout all our incarnations, and the way in which we dealt with those adversities, are preparation for the achievement of the ultimate goal of the Kingdom of Heaven. The procedure can be compared with the many tortuous processes through which steel passes before it becomes the finished product and can be regarded as 'true as steel'.

The Leader of Plane Six is another Greek and his name is Tomas. The Greeks appear to be prominent in being Plane Leaders because of their great understanding of life, existence and spiritual matters.

The Greek philosophers, thinkers and academics already mentioned had considerable knowledge of eternity and Socrates was judicially murdered for his understanding of life beyond the physical universe. Civilizations that are thousands of years old can teach Western society much in matters spiritual but religions, with their fake and insidious dogmas, spoil any chance of the real truth coming to light.

My wonderful, faithful, Guide, who is my soulmate, once took me astral travelling to Plane Six. For those who are not sure what that means, I had an out-of-body travel. It is a place of indescribable beauty but I shall do my best to explain what I saw.

The first thing that I saw was a magnificent marble building like a University with wide steps ascending to the entrance, something like the steps leading up to St Paul's Cathedral in London. There were marble pillars the whole length of the building and the roof was in the shape of a shell-like scroll.

I was told that this was the main building on Plane Six where the great philosophers meet and talk and indeed, while I watched, scholarly figures were to be seen entering and leaving the building. They were dressed in ancient Greek-fashioned robes, some carrying books that looked quite heavy, while others had scrolls of manuscripts in their hands. There was an atmosphere of great peace, calm, quiet and wisdom. I particularly noticed this after the noise and bustle of Earth.

We moved on, my Guide and I, to see fountains playing in the beautiful gardens outside the building. The crystal-clear water contained fish with brilliant multicoloured scales and they came to me when I put my hand in the water. They did not dart away in fear but seemed to 'speak' to me welcoming me and I could understand them. It was truly a heavenly experience!

As I love a beautiful garden, I took particular notice of the lovely roses planted in neat, tidy beds. I cannot describe the colours but one rose was blue in colour. I was thrilled to see such splendour before me; all the colours familiar to us on Earth were portrayed in the flowers that I saw, only they were more beautiful still. The grass was cut short and was like velvet upon which to walk. It was green but a green that we cannot imagine while incarnate.

I was completely awe-struck and, of course, did not want to leave. Who would? However, I had to be content with a tiny glimpse of Paradise and return to stark reality once more, by returning to my physical body. This little trip cheered me up considerably and helped me to face the daily, drab, domestic chores of my busy life.

Religion and prayers are unnecessary in the Kingdom of Heaven because the inhabitants have progressed, spiritually, beyond the need for either. Everyone has accepted total responsibility for himself or herself, kharma has been completed, all kharmic debts have been paid and there is no further risk of reincarnation, *unless* one is asked by the Spiritual Hierarchy to return to Earth for a special mission.

Inhabitants of Planes Five and Six *are* likely to be asked by the Spiritual Hierarchy to reincarnate for a reason. Jesus Christ was on Plane Five, having lived eleven lives and completed His kharma, when He was approached by one of God's Messengers, called Gabriel, and asked if He would reincarnate to do a very special job. I shall deal with this in greater detail later.

Plane Five is the last preparation ground in Heaven for the Kingdom of Heaven. When one reaches Plane Five, any rough edges that might be left in a spiritual being's thinking are smoothed over and the finished, polished spiritual being can now enter Plane Six.

Sometimes, if there is only a little atonement left for a spiritual being to complete, it is possible to finish the atonement on Plane Five. For example, a spiritual being can act as a Guide to someone on Earth. If the spiritual being does a good job and gives faithful service to the incarnate person, he can then progress to the Kingdom of Heaven having finished all atonement.

All Plane Six, Kingdom of Heaven personnel are educated, disciplined, responsible, ethical people who are beyond reproach. Their thinking equals their exemplary behaviour. There is no need for any of them to glorify God because they already have a tremendous respect for Him. Hymn singing, the chanting of mantras and reading from the Bible are obsolete activities in the Kingdom of Heaven.

This may sound peculiar but it is true. People have been led to believe that those who have evolved highly spend their time singing God's praises, playing harps and flitting between Heaven and Earth using a pair of huge white wings. As movement in Heaven is by a thought process, this makes the use of wings completely unnecessary.

In the Great Main Hall, like a University of which I spoke earlier in this lesson, there are libraries filled from floor to ceiling with leather-bound books on all kinds of learned subjects. Debates and discussions are held here and musical concerts such as operas, symphony concerts and great oratorios are played and sung. Life is full of light, colour, beauty, peace and harmony. No one *ever* has any negative thoughts or feelings.

Just in case students should think, "Well, an oratorio is usually a biblical story set to music," yes, this may be so but, the oratorios that are presented were heavenly-inspired works anyway, and Haydn's *The Creation* tells the story of the Creation. Handel's oratorio *The Messiah* told the story of Jesus Christ's coming. Both composers were inspired and religiously minded, therefore their works were bound to include a certain religious element. *The Crucifixion* is not a popular work and is omitted from the repertoire. This is out of consideration for Jesus Christ.

When one has reached the Kingdom of Heaven, one realizes the futility of religions as they are practised on Earth and the greater is the realization that belief in, and the practise of, religion of any denomination are totally unnecessary. Many religious leaders of the past, who have been most highly revered, have been astounded to learn, upon their arrival in Heaven, that, far from being greeted by God and Jesus Christ, they have incurred a return ticket to Earth.

I have spoken with many occupants of the Kingdom of Heaven in my research. Every one of them has told me that since entering Heaven they have had to change their religious ideas and thinking if they wanted to get anywhere spiritually, which they did.

Studious-minded people naturally want to progress to the limit and cannot rest until they reach the set goal.

That goal, Plane Six, the Kingdom of Heaven, is certainly worth striving for but the path to it is far from easy.

The Chart of Spiritual Existence — Part Two

Brilliant white auras	**SPHERE EIGHT** The Gardeners of the Earth The Government of the Universe
GOD — His aura is purple and gold	**PLANE SEVEN** The House of God Senior High Spiritual Beings
Deep blue auras	**PLANE SIX** The Kingdom of Heaven
Blue and yellow auras	**PLANE FIVE** The Plane of No Return
Multicoloured auras	**PLANE FOUR** The Graduation Plane
Green and yellow auras	**PLANE THREE**
Green auras	**PLANE TWO** The Threshold of Spiritual Awakening

PLANE ONE
-- or --
The Astral

Brown auras varying in shade

Dark brown auras

Upper Astral

Lower Astral

Lesson 10 Part Two

JESUS CHRIST – THE TRUTH

In my last lesson, I stated that Jesus Christ was on Plane Five in Heaven when He was approached by God's Messenger, Gabriel, and asked if He would return to Earth to do a particularly hazardous job. Jesus Christ had lived eleven lives and had finished His kharma but He expressed interest in this special task, so Gabriel took Him along to meet God on Plane Seven.

God outlined the work that the Lord God in Sphere Eight wanted Jesus Christ to do and pointed out that, after due consideration of His previous life history, the Lord God and He, God, had decided that Jesus Christ was the best man for the job.

Jesus Christ agreed to tackle what must have seemed the impossible to Him but, being a stalwart gentleman and knowing that He would have the backing of very High Spiritual Beings, He was briefed for His forthcoming incarnation.

It *is* possible for Jesus Christ to communicate directly with incarnate people and I have read one or two accounts of this happening. I have no reason to doubt the authenticity of these accounts because of the way in which they were related and written. The circumstances which led up to the events that were described by the authors, were absolutely feasible. Possibly there are many more accounts somewhere but the people concerned are afraid to come out into the open about them for fear of being ridiculed and, worse still, hounded by religious fanatics.

Jesus Christ is a spiritual being, as we all are, therefore it is not unreasonable to assume that He is capable of communicating with incarnate people just the same as any other spiritual being in Heaven could communicate with incarnate persons.

Again, people have been led to believe, quite falsely, by religious leaders, that *no one* on Earth can be spoken to directly by Jesus Christ. They have put Him on such a high pedestal that most people consider that Jesus Christ is out of their reach and can only be approached through prayer. This is not true, as I have proved.

I mentioned very early on in the Course that like attracts like and, as Jesus Christ did not come into this world in order to *start* a religion, the last person with whom He would be likely to communicate is anyone who is deeply religious or heavily biased towards any one faith. An interview with a person thus inclined would be full of religious aberration and a clear account of the occasion would be impossible.

As I have been consciously aware all through this present life of mine that there was more to life and eternity than meets the eye, I continually strove for something better and, ten years ago, I found it after much seeking. Although I was brought up as a Methodist, I only paid lip service to it to please my dear grandfather who is now on Plane Five. Needless to say that he, too, has seen the light about religions!

I was talking with my Guide one day when he hesitated slightly. Sensing that something was afoot, I enquired what it was. My Guide said, "A Very Important Person wishes to speak to you." Excitedly, I said, "Oh, tell me quickly who it is." I could not believe my ears when Jesus Christ Himself, in Person, spoke to me. I was filled with awe and surprise but He soon put me at my ease. The Great Man politely enquired after my health and introduced Himself.

I did not see Him right away, that immense honour came later. I was very aware of His wonderful, peaceful Presence and, of course, we conversed telepathically as I do with all my spiritual friends. Jesus Christ told me that He had heard of my strong interest in spiritual matters and that I had a very enquiring mind that could pierce myths, legends and beliefs! We laughed.

He then proceeded to ask me many questions about spiritual matters and the spiritual existence. He seemed very pleased with my answers and the manner in which I answered them. It became obvious that I was being tested on my knowledge of both. Jesus Christ then took His leave but said that He would return as He required me to do a job for Him. So began a remarkable chain of events.

I wondered what was required of me. I did not have long to wait in order to find out. Jesus Christ returned a few days later and said that He wished to write a chapter through me correcting many details regarding Him and His work. I was surprised because I had always thought, as millions of other people do, that the bible was infallible and that we already had the truth. How wrong I was!

Jesus Christ and I worked hard together for many days. I sat with pen and paper leaving my mind open for His use. He wrote, telling me when to rest and when to take refreshment. One does tend to become so engrossed that time and all material things are forgotten. Jesus Christ always introduced Himself in the same manner each time, namely, "I, Jesus Christ of Nazareth and Calvary...." As He wrote through me, I felt as though I had been transported back in time to those days when He lived on this Earth. I was there following and witnessing every move. It was an astonishing experience. Here is that script.

> I, Jesus Christ of Nazareth and Calvary, do hereby state that I am writing this through Amanda Valiant. In an attempt to clarify certain events and straighten the records once and for all, I have been fortunate in securing a mind that is completely free from bias, religious or otherwise, the mind of Amanda Valiant, a High Spiritual Being incarnate. It is not possible, in one chapter, to cover everything concerning my last incarnation, therefore I have selected some salient aspects.
>
> I had completed my kharma, having lived eleven lives, nine of which were spent on the planet Earth in different eras. I was a High Spiritual Being residing on Plane Five in Heaven, when I was approached by another High Spiritual Being called Gabriel and asked if I would be willing to return to Earth to perform a very special task.
>
> I was given the outline of the mission which, to me,

sounded quite a challenge and I accepted it confidently. Gabriel, it seemed, was a member of God's staff and he showed me into His presence. God congratulated me for accepting the mission and reminded me that it would not be an easy one.

He went on to explain that He had been communicated with by the 'High Ones', as He called the Gardeners of the Earth, and asked to choose a suitably qualified male, spiritual being and brief him for a difficult and hazardous incarnation. Therefore, I was sent to Earth by the Gardeners of the Earth and NOT by God.

My task was to introduce spiritual matters to the peoples of the time who were particularly ignorant of such things. I was intended to awaken their interest in the power of the mind, the importance of spiritual values in everyday living and, especially, in the life after death which is absolutely certain. No person can cease to exist by dying. Only the physical body decays and dies.

I wish to explain the real truth behind my existence on Earth almost two thousand years ago. I was born, in the usual way, of Joseph and Mary. My mother was not a virgin as I was her third child. It is a well-known fact, in your modern times, that a virgin birth, which is extremely rare, produces only a female child.

A virgin birth is one that has occurred without the introduction of male genes and is an event known as parthenogenesis. It is caused by a foreign particle in the womb which slightly scratches the ovum. This stimulates the initial subdivision of the ovum thereby initiating the subsequent, automatic multiplication of the cells. Owing to the entire absence of male genes, it is impossible for a male child to result. This happening has been the cause of much distress to the unfortunate girls who, of course, were immediately accused of immorality when they became pregnant.

There was nothing mysterious about my conception

and birth and all stories of my mother being 'conceived of the Holy Ghost' are nonsense and a myth created by religious leaders to try to impress the ignorant.

The story of my being born in a stable is true, so also is the fact that Herod was very keen to know of my whereabouts. The three 'Wise Men' were ordinary travelling merchants, going about their business, who just happened to be in the right place at the right time to report on what they had seen. The 'star' which hovered over the stable at the time of my birth, was a materialized spiritual spaceship. This spaceship belongs to, and is piloted by, the Lord God in Sphere Eight. I shall be referring to Him several times as I am a kinsman of His. I live in Sphere Eight but I work with God and His helpers on Plane Seven. I liaise between the Heavenly Hierarchy and all the other Planes in Heaven.

To move on a few years, I did address the officials in the temple and they marvelled at my knowledge for one so young. I was, of course, being helped greatly by High Spiritual Beings in the spiritual world.

When I was thirteen years old, I was met by a Messenger from the Lord God's spaceship. His name was Zaugel. He told me who I really was and what I was on Earth to do. I already knew from my father, Joseph, that I was on Earth for a very special reason for he was a strong psychic. Until I was thirteen, I had no real idea of what I was expected to do. Then, I was taken by Zaugel into a 'flying machine' for want of a better description. It was made of a bright silvery metal and was circular in plan. Its shape, in fact, agreed very much with the modern concept of a 'flying saucer'. A ladder enabled us to enter in the centre underneath the craft which was about ten metres in diameter. Once inside, still wearing my cotton garment, I felt very cold, although outside, the sun was scorching and the sand burned my feet through the soles of my leather sandals.

Inside, I was introduced to other people who looked

like young men to me. I was more interested than afraid and was soon made to feel at ease by being given good food and drink. About an hour later, my task was explained to me in detail and I was told that we were to fly to a land, at the other side of the world, where I would be educated and trained in preparation for my return to Israel to commence my vital work.

The journey itself was fascinating. There was a window in the bottom of the spacecraft through which I was allowed to view the world passing beneath me. We were only in the air about two hours but we did not fly very high above the earth. There was a tremendous, roaring noise at take-off but, once we were up at a fair height, all noise ceased and everything was unusually quiet.

My 'abductors', if I may use the word, kept me interested and treated me very kindly but entirely without any sense of reverence or deference. Our destination was the Indian continent. During the landing, there was a great rushing sound again and, when it started, I was very frightened. I was soon pacified and the flying machine landed gently, the engines died away and I was led outside into brilliant sunshine again. Thus began the monastic education of me, Jesus Christ.

Until I was twenty-nine years old, I worked extremely hard at my studies, under a very strict discipline, that of the Essene Order, renowned for their correct living and thinking at that time. I was, at first, treated like all the other monks but, for the last five years of my training, I was virtually alone except for my teachers.

When I finished my education at the monastery, I was given a strict examination and told that I had the important task of educating the people in the land of my birth in spiritual matters. It was arranged that I should reappear in Israel and start my mission. I was given no money and no possessions with which to ease my burdens and was simply transported in a spacecraft by the same crew as brought me to India, back to Israel, only this time we landed at night behind some hills.

I was asked to leave the craft and start my work immediately. This I did. I walked into Jerusalem and began begging in order to live. I never worked regularly for a living but I was taught carpentry by my father Joseph and, later, in the monastery. I used to do odd jobs to earn the price of a meal occasionally. After several months had passed, I had attracted a great deal of attention and some followers or disciples who stayed with me and helped me in my work of lecturing. I also held public meetings in order to put my message across.

In my lectures to the public while I toured Israel, I referred to the spiritual God. I knew that 'gods' had been visiting Earth for centuries. Their spacecraft are described in the bible by Abraham, Moses and Ezekiel among other references. All three of these great spiritual beings are now Gardeners of the Earth.

In order to put the record straight, I should like to state that Ezekiel's book in the bible is in the wrong place chronologically. There are numerous mistakes in the bible. Some are accidental, others are errors in translation but the great tragedy of the bible is the way it has been distorted by Christian prelates throughout the ages.

If only they had left the books alone, there might have been a greater degree of success for me but, because they simply failed to understand most of what I said, they altered it, or left it out. All references to spacecraft were deleted from those sayings of mine that were recorded by my disciples. The only vehicle known in those days was the cart or chariot, so I used the words 'chariot of the skies'. When trying to communicate with primitive people, I had to resort to the parable since it was the only way I could illustrate my meanings. You will realize that most people, except those in authority, were illiterate. The average vocabulary in those days would not have exceeded about three hundred words, so I had great difficulty in putting my meanings across. That I succeeded with some is something of which I still feel proud.

Most of the stories in the bible concerning my healing people are true except that the healing was coming from two High Spiritual Beings in Sphere Eight. I merely acted as a medium to make those things possible. The story of the loaves and fishes was exaggerated out of all proportion. What, in fact, happened was that there were about fifty people by the sea who complained to me that they were hungry. One of the powers given to me to help me in my work was that of the ability to create matter spontaneously. I created by thought postulate fifty fish and a few loaves of bread. These were materialized and the crowd ate them. This may seem like a miracle to most people but it is a phenomenon that is not restricted to my use alone. Others have been able, using considerable spiritual power, to materialize living things or inanimate objects.

The brief mention in John, chapter two, of the bible regarding the miracle of turning water into wine at the wedding feast, is based on an actual event but, as so often happened, it was misunderstood and poorly reported. The wedding feast had been under way for some hours and most of the guests were intoxicated, with the exception of my mother, my disciples and myself, who had all drunk wine in moderation. My mother quietly told me that the wine had almost run out and asked me if I could do anything about it.

I commanded the servants to fill water pots to the brim and bring them into the hall. I addressed the people present and, by the force of my personality, was able to implant a strong positive suggestion that the water pots contained a high quality wine.

It is a well-known fact in present-day society that a hypnotist can implant thoughts into people's minds for them to do or say certain things and then, later, to forget what happened. I used the same technique and as each person dipped his cup into the water pot, I touched him and reinforced the positive suggestion that he was about to drink wine.

Anyone who has witnessed a demonstration of hypnosis will know that a hypnotized person given water to drink while being told it is gin, for example, will behave as though drunk. Low Spiritual Beings are easily influenced and can be readily hypnotized.

The sermon on the Mount was delivered by me to try to educate the primitive people. In my humble way I was trying to set a moral standard by which they should live, as Moses tried to do with the Israelites before me.

Now I will deal with my crucifixion. I failed in my mission on Earth. I feel that I have been responsible for the suffering and cruelty of others who have died defending my name. Things started to go wrong when I was arrested and taken before Pontius Pilate. He was a fair man and not a wicked ruler but he was under great pressure from political groups to get rid of me because I represented a threat to them. He finally relented and washed his hands symbolically and literally. The bloodthirsty crowds just wanted to see a man crucified, any man would do and any reason would do.

I did NOT die to save anybody. In fact, I did NOT die on the cross at Calvary at all! Although I was wounded by a spear thrust into my side by a Roman soldier, I survived. I did not carry the whole of my own cross, only the crossbeam. Simon of Cyrene was allowed to assist me, as a complete, heavy, wooden cross would have been far too weighty for one man to lift, even for me. The three crosses were laid side-by-side on the ground. The criminals and I were fixed to them and they were erected into an upright position.

Later, I was taken down unconscious from the cross and pronounced dead by the Roman legionary. My body was laid in a tomb owned by Joseph of Arimathea.

Joseph wrapped my body in a shroud that he was keeping for his own body. This shroud is still in existence today and is known as the Turin Shroud which is, at intervals, put on public display.

The extraordinary imprint of my body upon it, which was discovered centuries later, is the work of the Lord God in Sphere Eight. He achieved this phenomenon by the use of spiritual radiation and this is why scientists, so far, have been baffled about its origin. Physical methods of investigation cannot be applied to spiritual phenomena.

Joseph of Arimathea's tomb consisted of several large white stones laid on top of one another. Finally, after my mother had left, presuming me dead, a large stone was rolled in front of the tomb to keep people out.

This is where the mind of the reader is going to be sorely tested because I, Jesus Christ of Nazareth and Calvary tell you that I was rescued, still alive, from that tomb by the Lord God and by Zaugel His Messenger. Zaugel, using tremendous spiritual power, rolled away the large stone that blocked the entrance to the tomb.

The reason that the guards did not realize that anything had happened is that they were made to fall asleep just long enough for Zaugel to pick me up and carry me away. Putting humans to sleep is a simple matter for those in Sphere Eight.

Now, we come to the episode which was completely deleted from the bible although there were witnesses present at the time. Zaugel carried me to the Lord God's spacecraft. Spacecraft have been in use for thousands of years and are still in use today. Many people have seen them but governments hide the truth and deny that they exist because they are afraid to let it be known that there could be a power in existence that is greater than their own.

After being laid in the spacecraft by Zaugel, I was immediately given healing by the two most powerful spiritual healers in the Universe. The spacecraft was flown to India where I rested for three days and was then flown back to Israel. The intention was for me to reappear before the Jewish people in order to demonstrate the great power of the spirit. This was, really, a last resort aimed at trying to retain some of the good work that I had done on Earth.

I was considerably weakened by my ordeal and it was decided that the Lord God and the two powerful healers would provide me with enough spiritual energy to materialize my spiritual body and reappear at Galilee. This was done. The wounds that I received at my crucifixion were still evident on my spiritual body in order to convince people as to my true identity. I then paraded my spiritual body in materialized form before the astonished crowds, while my physical body lay in the well-hidden spacecraft.

It was possible for me to speak while thus materialized and I continued to appear before various people. Then, I returned to my physical body and appeared, to the public, to vanish for the second time.

The spacecraft was then flown to India again, where I recovered fully from my crucifixion and lived to the age of seventy-two years. I travelled extensively in Eastern and Asiatic countries after my recovery and my travels have been documented by other authors. I eventually died of natural causes.

Matthew has faithfully reported in his gospel in the bible, the bribery and corruption of the chief priests and elders of my day. They called me a 'deceiver' and were responsible for bribing the soldiers, who were on duty at my tomb, to tell everyone that my disciples had stolen my body during the night and hidden it.

Christianity today is an absolute shambles and bears little or no relationship to my teachings when I was in Israel. I did not 'invent' Christianity. In fact, it was not intended that I should start a religion at all. The *whole* point of my being on Earth was to educate people in the art of spiritual development. No amount of petty atonement such as is practised by Catholics can ever make the slightest difference to the spiritual state of a human being. Neither can self-inflicted pain, using flagellation or other means, have the slightest effect other than to harm the performer of it.

I state, categorically, that I am NOT the Son of God, neither am I God. I am Jesus Christ, a man born like any other man and who died like any other man. God did NOT send His only begotten son to Earth because God has no son and cannot, as a Spiritual Being, possibly have one. I am not holy or divine, since these words mean absolutely nothing to anyone on the higher planes of Heaven.

I am a Gardener of the Earth, an appointment which was my reward for the service that I rendered mankind in my last life. I am very happy working with the other Gardeners and with God, still for the good of mankind.

I cannot thank my 'instrument', Amanda Valiant, enough for allowing me the opportunity to speak freely and to correct the harm that has been done to my teachings and work since I was last incarnate. I hope that in writing this chapter I shall have helped to bring about a turning-point in the spiritual evolution of the peoples of Earth.

When one studies the life and work of Jesus Christ, it can easily be seen that He was one of the finest spiritual mediums who ever walked this Earth. The Dead Sea scrolls contain much of the real truth about Jesus Christ's life and work. For instance, He taught the facts about reincarnation but this was suppressed by the religious officials of the period for political reasons and jealousy. Someone was on Earth who knew more than they did and who was attracting a great deal more attention than they were receiving. It had to stop!

Really, little has changed today, for when anyone tries to

teach something revolutionary and it is for good, pressure is exerted to try to squash it. However, truth *will* out in one way or another!

When we had finished our task, Jesus Christ read through our efforts, checking and re-checking the work until He was satisfied that we had got it right. At last, we were both very pleased with the result and the Great Man congratulated me on my ability to concentrate for long periods of time on such exacting work. I said that I was greatly honoured to be able to do it for Him.

He tried to explain life in the spiritual world as it *really* is and not as it has been presented in the past by charlatans, pompous clerics and by those who did not understand. He laid great stress upon the importance of each human being's spiritual development and progress. There are no short cuts to salvation and no one can work out your salvation for you.

Please refer to the full Chart, included in Lesson 9, throughout Part Two of the Course.

Lesson 11   **Part Two**

GOD'S ROLE IN THE UNIVERSE

After the privilege of speaking to Jesus Christ in Person, I then considered the possibility of being able to talk to His so-called 'Father', God. After all I thought, in a family, when one has met one member of it, one is normally introduced to the rest of them. I did not consider this idea to be unreasonable or too preposterous and my wonderful Guide and Soulmate, who has stuck by me through thick and thin, agreed with my thoughts.

God lives and works on Plane Seven in Heaven. *He* is in charge of this Plane which is a very exclusive one. Only a few very specially chosen High Spiritual Beings live on Plane Seven with Him. At intervals, God travels through all the seven planes of Heaven incognito. I learned from my Guide and Soulmate that this was a necessary precaution for such a High Personage, otherwise He would be besieged by spiritual beings all pleading for forgiveness and asking that their sins be absolved and so on because this is what they were taught, when incarnate, to expect of God.

My Guide and Soulmate resides on Plane Seven in his own house there so he knows God very well indeed. A meeting between God and insignificant me — as I thought then — was arranged. I did not see God at first. I was only very much aware of His Great Presence as I heard Him speak and was overcome with awe and guilt for things that I had said and done in this present life of mine that I would have given anything to wipe out.

God called me by name. I sat bolt upright with incredulity in spite of my earlier thoughts of expectation to speak with Him! I gasped, "Great heavens, God speaking to little me!" Then I began fervently to apologize for the indiscretions in my life, and for the things that I had done which I realized, years later, were wrong. I said, "God, Sir, I have done wrong but I am desperately trying to put it all right." His reply was, "My dear child, you cannot do any more than you are already doing." Thus began a clairaudient, two-way conversation between God and me which has led to a deep affinity and understanding that are impossible, adequately, to describe.

God speaks in a very well-modulated and cultured voice. In fact, my very first thought on hearing Him speak was that He had been educated at Eton! No offence is meant or implied by this remark and, when I got to know God a bit better, we both laughed at my cheeky but humorous comparison of His voice.

We talked together many times on a variety of subjects and some of the subjects we discussed will be included in this lesson. During our conversations, God told me that His Purpose is to see that everyone completes their kharma, to control the genetic line of the human and animal kingdoms, (genetic engineering scientists please note), and to clear this planet of its evil. The latter appears to be a forlorn hope until everyone understands the contents of this vital Course.

I learned that God can be gentle, kind, loving, understanding and considerate, yet He can, when the occasion warrants it, be stern, unrelenting and formidable. In order to do His vital work, He *must* be absolutely impartial or He could not perform the crucial task that He has been given by Another. This will be explained in a future lesson.

I also discovered during my talks with God that He is an entirely different Being from that preached about by religions and priests. I found that their concepts of Him are completely wrong. For instance, God has *never* been incarnate. He is a Very High Spiritual Being living on Plane Seven in Heaven. He has the spiritual body of a man but His Mind is unique and infinitely superior.

He is not an Almighty Deity sitting on a resplendent throne in Heaven, surrounded by a blinding light and handing out terrible punishments to shivering mortals brought before Him. People earn their own rewards or punishments as explained in Lesson 4 on Kharma and Reincarnation.

God has a good sense of humour, a wonderful compassion for all human and animal life, yet feels a deep sadness to see men destroying themselves with greed and enmity towards one another. Once we are put on this planet Earth, we are responsible for ourselves. God is *not* responsible for us or the things that we do, neither does He control us. It is wrong to blame God for nearly everything that does not meet with our approval. God washes His hands of us once we are here although a few selected mortals may receive special, spiritual attention. Many are called, few are chosen and even fewer stand the pace expected of them.

As time passed and a marvellous affinity between us had been established, I had the temerity to ask God if He would like to write through me, an unworthy servant but a willing one. He very graciously accepted the invitation and here is the result of our work together. God has covered a variety of subjects, His views upon which He felt would be most beneficial to erring man, as he is very cognisant of what is happening in this world today.

This is God writing through Amanda Valiant

I am *not* the father of Jesus Christ. He is not *My* Son. The pious belief in the immaculate or divine conception is entirely unfounded and erroneous. It stemmed, in fact, from earlier prophecies that originated in India.

Jesus Christ does *not* intercede with Me on behalf of people and the sentence, 'Through Jesus Christ our Lord. . . . ' is utterly meaningless. Everyone is responsible for their own actions, thoughts and deeds and is rewarded or punished accordingly by Me.

I should like to define the word 'holy'. In the Old Testament of the bible, Moses saw a burning bush. This illusion was caused by a spaceship landing and taking off making the ground around it very hot, therefore anyone stepping on the ground would be very severely burnt. In order to avoid this, the ground was labelled 'forbidden' by the Officer-in-Charge of Sphere Eight who piloted the spaceship. The word 'forbidden' has been incorrectly translated as 'holy'.

I did not create Heaven and Earth. I am not Almighty, as the church preaches. I do not have *full* control over the elements. I receive periodic instructions from Sphere Eight and I control the genetic lines of the human and animal kingdoms and people's kharmas.

Omnipotent does not apply to Me because I am not all-powerful. Omnipresent *is* applicable to Me because My Mind *is* everywhere at once. As God, My Mind is as no one in a physical body can comprehend, therefore it is impossible to explain to an incarnate person how My Mind is omnipresent. They cannot understand their own minds, let alone Mine! Omniscient does not apply to Me, either, but I *do* possess tremendous knowledge and ability. 'God is love?' Yes, I, God, am full of love for people.

Kharma

This has already been explained. I only wish to add that the best way to work out one's kharma is to be as kind, thoughtful to others, pleasant, loving and pure in heart, mind and spirit as possible. This is very difficult under conditions prevailing on Earth *but not impossible.* Every wicked and destructive deed, word or thought results in punishment of one kind or another which can carry on from lifetime to lifetime, for you live many lives.

Reincarnation

Reincarnation is the occupation of a new physical body by a spiritual being. I, God, do not create a new spiritual being for each new physical body and babies are not born completely innocent. This is explained under the next heading.

Atonement

This is the clearing of crimes or sins committed *in all one's incarnate, human existence.* The clearing process may take several lives depending on how good or bad a person is. A good person could complete his atonement in, say, twelve lives, living an average of seventy years in each life. Whereas a bad person could take seven thousand incarnate years to clear his atonement, living seventy years in each life for one hundred lives. The crimes to which I refer are not necessarily punishable by Earth law but may be transgressions of the spiritual laws, which exist in Heaven. Heaven must have its laws too, just the same as Earth, in order to preserve the smooth running of the Universe.

Man

I am now going to define man. He, and this applies to women and children as well, not just the male species, consists of two bodies. One is the spiritual body which lives in several different physical bodies in separate lifetimes on Earth. The other is the physical body which houses the spiritual body while it is incarnate.

The computer for the physical body is the BRAIN which controls all the physical functions of the human body. The computer for the spiritual body is the MIND which is non-physical and which is the subject of much speculation in the psychiatric world. A human being on Earth is, therefore, MIND AND SPIRITUAL BODY, BRAIN AND PHYSICAL BODY.

The spiritual body can be temporarily separated from the physical body, together with the mind. This is called astral travelling by some people or exteriorization by others. While the spiritual body is exterior, it is still connected to its physical body by a silver cord, through which the mind influences the physical body and vice versa, just as a baby is still connected to its mother's body by a cord at birth. The spiritual body and the mind can be separated from the physical body permanently. This process is known as death. Only the physical body decays.

Poltergeists

These very low spiritual beings on the Lower Astral, can cause considerable havoc in the physical world of Earth by throwing or moving objects about. They are also capable of causing immense damage and suffering by influencing the minds of incarnate people, telepathically. It has already been stressed in earlier lessons by Amanda, how important it is to have a thorough understanding of the spiritual world. I reinforce this instruction because like *does* attract like. Those who play with fire must expect to get burnt unless they fully understand how to handle it.

Some poltergeists are incarnate and only exist to destroy and cause as much trouble as possible. Strikers are usually whipped up into action by these low beings, who are so clever about it that they have no difficulty in getting the weak-minded to follow them. They get a great kick out of mistakenly thinking that they have thwarted My Purpose. However, none escapes their just punishment.

Punishments

I have plenty of these and here are some of them. Insanity, mysterious diseases, damaged organs, deformities, loss of sight or hearing and unpleasant deaths. The severity of these afflictions can be varied according to the degree of wickedness. People get what they deserve and, here again, a person may be suffering in his present life for crimes committed in two or more lifetimes previously.

Rewards

On the other hand, however, when a person at last shows interest in becoming a good spirit, is truly repentant and has atoned, then the rewards are great. Here is a short list of rewards: good health, happiness, successful business, a general sense of well-being, comfortable living standards, perhaps even riches and living a well-ordered and satisfying life. All well worth striving for.

Sin

Sin is a word used by religions to describe crimes. There are two basic types of sin, against yourself, and against others. The sin against oneself is to allow one's own high spiritual state and intelligent mind to be corrupted by involvement in undesirable practices such as drug-taking, witchcraft, debauchery, drunkenness and gluttony. Sins against others include the following: stealing, vandalism, injury causing grievous bodily harm, causing mental suffering by suppression, defamation of character, blackmail, extortion, cheating and telling lies.

Blood Sports

Blood sports are particularly abominable because innocent and defenceless animals are hunted down for 'pleasure', which to Me, God, is barbarity. On the other hand, it is not a sin to hunt for food in order to survive, provided the animal being hunted is humanely and quickly despatched with the minimum of suffering.

Perversions, Marriage and Divorce

The rape and sexual perversion of adults and children constitute serious sexual crimes. They are all the more pernicious when the innocence and immaturity of the victims are exploited. Homosexuality and lesbianism between consenting persons are not crimes. However, this kind of relationship between people is not desirable and should be discouraged because it helps to lower the moral standards of society.

It is not a sin for a man and a woman to live together without being married. Here, again, this kind of relationship is not desirable and should be discouraged, not only because it contributes to the moral decline of society but many complications arise if one partner decides to leave the other after children have resulted from the union. The children are immediately deprived of a parent and this is bad for them.

A full and complete family life, lived in an atmosphere of love for one another, parents and children alike, are what I, God, want to see in every household.

Desertion and divorce happen in the marital state too, but longer courtships should help to prevent breakdowns of marriage. Getting to know one another more thoroughly before entering into such an important contract as marriage results in greater confidence. A longer period of courtship will, naturally, mean a certain strain on the emotions but self-control and self-discipline can be cultivated, as can patience, understanding and mutual respect. Any relationship between two people that is not founded upon mutual respect is liable to fall asunder, sooner or later. Further, indulging in similar interests and hobbies and studying the marital state diligently, leads to a better understanding of the marriage contract.

In order to accomplish anything worth while, successfully, study and practice are necessary but few people realize that living in the married state is an art that must be worked at. There are many excellent books on marriage written by experienced authors who give sensible advice. A small sum invested in such books, *before* marriage, is well spent, as is the time taken in studying them. These precautions are infinitely preferable to the terrible heartbreak of disastrous years spent together or an irretrievable breakdown of the union.

The Papacy

The pope is definitely NOT My Representative on Earth. No one is. In fact, all ex-popes, upon their return to Heaven, are informed at a suitable stage in their re-education, that they must return to Earth in order to do a useful job of work and contribute to the welfare of their community in a practical, helpful way instead of spending their lives deeply involved in a false religion, misguiding millions of people. Then, without exception, they are reincarnated into the much less pompous jobs of life such as farm labourers, road sweepers, mine workers and even dustmen!

The Bible

A few words now on the bible. First of all, nothing that is written in the bible was written by Me or even inspired by Me. Numerous psychic events recorded therein did actually happen but many other incidents reported are the result of distorted messages carried by word of mouth and of the embellishment of ordinary happenings so as to create a religious mystique.

Clergymen study the bible, archbishops expound upon it, lay preachers preach from it, the population read it, but none understands it. They are not to be blamed, however. The real culprits, the priests of the Convocation in AD 268, have been suitably dealt with by Me for destroying the vital facts and evidence that should have remained in the bible. There is *some* truth in the bible but it needs a great deal of sifting.

The Church

I, God, have *no* church. All people who say that they have a 'calling' to enter the church are experiencing a subconscious reality of the life they led in Heaven between incarnations. They *know* that there is a spiritual existence, with Me very much in evidence. They are anxious to get My message through to others but, unfortunately, they go about it in a misguided fashion. This is owing to the fact that, in early childhood, people are wrongly taught the fundamentals of spirituality which are grossly misunderstood by practitioners of religions.

Missionaries do wonderful work as long as they restrict their activities to giving practical help where it is needed. As soon as they present the religious aspects, they spoil everything for themselves and for the people whom they are trying to help.

I do not want to be worshipped or praised in churches because that implies that I am infinitely vain. All I want is for people to live together peacefully and work out their kharmas. The *real* truth about Jesus Christ and Me was suppressed in AD 268 by the Elders of the Church. There was no effective government at that time and hardly any law, other than religious law, the church ruled the people by threat of hell-fire and damnation if they did not do as the church dictated.

My views on a welfare state are that any Welfare State is a bad thing in some respects, as it robs people of their independence and self-determinism. People are led to believe that the State will do everything for them from the cradle to the grave and this creates a vicious circle.

Some people do not *want* to work and those who *do* wish to earn an honest living often find that it does not pay them to do so because of the 'system'. Too much reliance by the individual upon the State leaves a country wide open to sedition.

I wrote more than this through Amanda Valiant but, for the purposes of this lesson, the details I have given are sufficient. I, God, am very pleased to have had this opportunity of expressing My True Self through an unbiased channel. I have no need to thank Amanda, she *understands.*

Naturally, God has a huge staff of High Spiritual Beings to help Him in His enormous task. They do not live on Plane Seven but come and go as required in the performance of their duties.

God hears all *individual* prayers. Mass prayers and those which are ritual in format are ignored by Him. God pays attention to the *individual* and for *what* that person is praying.

This explains why some prayers are answered and some are not. Perhaps someone is being too selfish or is asking for something that is not good for them, or is not permitted for kharmic reasons. Perhaps a person is praying for the impossible, even! However, rest assured that your individual, *sincere* prayer *is* heard and considered by God.

My reward for all this tremendous work with God was an astral travel to Plane Seven, which was an enthralling experience. My Guide and Soulmate took me to see his own house which was a typical bachelor abode but very elegant and comfortable. Then, I was taken to see God's palace.

This was a magnificent sight which I shall *try* to describe *and* do it justice. It was a very large two-storey building in the shape of a half-moon and its style was Georgian with pillars and steps leading up to the entrance. The garden was, excuse the pun, a truly heavenly sight with neat lawns, flower beds filled with all kinds of beautiful blooms. Brightly coloured birds sang in the trees and fountains played and sparkled in glorious light.

My Guide and I went inside. We stood in a huge, marble hall which was coloured a wonderful green. It was not a jade green but a green that I have never seen, I can only say that it was breathtakingly wonderful!

There was a huge, marble staircase in the same colour as the hall, everything matched, and several brilliantly lit, crystal chandeliers hung from the ceiling. We passed through a long corridor beautifully decorated and carpeted, with magnificent pictures hanging on the walls. These pictures were painted by several great masters of bygone years. I recognized Constable's work and Leonardo da Vinci's 'Mona Lisa', the latter was prominently displayed.

There were rooms leading off from the corridor on both sides and here, in this corridor hurrying towards me, came another Very High Spiritual Being who was introduced to me as The Lord God, but this is described in another lesson.

PLANE SEVEN
God Reigns Here
Huge Staff of High Spiritual Beings work here but do not live here
Jesus Christ works but does not live here

God shares Plane Seven with only four other High Spiritual Beings who have, through several lifetimes of selfless devotion and by special merit, warranted and gained entry into God's Own Kingdom. I have been asked by God to withhold the names of the chosen four.

Lesson 12   **Part Two**

SPHERE EIGHT AND THE LORD GOD

Further surprises were in store for me after my initial meetings and conversations with God and Jesus Christ. I was curious to know more about the 'High Ones' to whom God was constantly referring whenever He had the opportunity to talk to me.

    I was recovering, slowly, from my illness which, I learned later on, was to have been my last and that the date set for me to leave this planet was 20th January, 1977. Throughout my sickness, I had been staying at a relative's house in town so that medical attention could be obtained more quickly.

    I was now asked by God to return to my home in the country and await further instructions, so my husband Alan and I duly journeyed back to the isolated domicile which was the home chosen for us by the 'High Ones' themselves, although we were unaware of this at the time.

    As my affinity with God and Jesus Christ was now quite firmly established and I regarded them both as very Dear Friends, it was not at all difficult to hold conversations with Them on a variety of subjects. When I was feeling strong enough to do so, I questioned God about the 'High Ones'. There was silence for a short while, then His answer came, "I will open the line for you, speak to Them yourself."

    Obviously, He had been given, or had sought, permission to do this. The time was ready for me to face 'The Great Unknown'. Seated at a table with paper and pen before me, my mind a complete blank and perfectly calm, the names of ten people were written. They were Archibald, Abraham, Isaac, Noah, Joseph, Moses, Ezekiel, Zaugel, Hildon and Gailbron.

    Then Archibald spoke to me. Calling me by my first name, He greeted me and told me that I had been spared for a while longer in order to perform a very special duty. Owing to my, and Alan's, exceptional understanding of the spiritual world and life in general, my task was to write a book giving the facts of existence in Heaven and on Earth and Alan was to help and support me.

By this time, I was thoroughly used to dealing with the unexpected and I politely asked who were the people whose names I had been given. I was told that they were the Gardeners of the Earth, the hierarchy of Heaven, and that their function was to govern the whole universe, both the spiritual one of Heaven in which they live and the physical one of Earth in which we live.

I was given the opportunity to back out of my task but an inborn sense of duty and responsibility stayed me. After agreeing to take on this momentous work, another surprise package was given to me — that I came from Sphere Eight! I am one of THEM! This explained why I was needed. At a conference of the Gardeners, it was unanimously agreed that I could, with massive spiritual help, do a great deal more while I was still incarnate and so, regretfully, the decision was made to keep me on Earth until this extra duty had been performed as satisfactorily as possible or until my health deteriorated so much that I was unable to do more.

In a sense, I, too, like Jesus Christ, have been rescued from the grave, a fact of which my physical body is a constant reminder with its ever-present aches and pains. In a sense, Alan and I feel rather like Aaron and Moses must have felt.

It is hoped that the information given in Part Two of this course will help to put some aspects of the bible into a better perspective. As Jesus Christ pointed out in Lesson Ten, there are many mistakes in the bible. Personally, I have always regarded it as a most confusing book, yet millions seem to base their whole lives and beliefs upon it. It is little wonder that so many are dissatisfied with the orthodox religions and are turning to other cults for the so-called 'guidance' they crave.

Each of the Gardeners of the Earth has written a script through me. Naturally, only the salient points can be discussed because of the enormity of the subjects. All the information from the hierarchy was received by me and by Alan, in the year 1977.

I now introduce the Gardeners of the Earth.

I am Archibald, the Officer-in-Charge of Sphere Eight, writing through Amanda Valiant. I gave God of Plane Seven instructions for Amanda and Alan to be guided to a quiet country residence in Cornwall, England, to live. The peaceful surroundings were perfect for inter-world communication as it was vital that we communicated with Amanda at the earliest opportunity. Both of them remarked, soon after their move to the house, that they felt they had been sent there for a purpose. They were right!

In her penultimate incarnation, Amanda was the only daughter of a high-ranking army officer, in Quebec, at the time of General Wolfe. She received an excellent education and upbringing, after which she attended a finishing school. Because of her very happy home life, her education, her altruistic behaviour and sensible attitudes towards life and people and, more importantly still, the advanced development of her spiritual evolution throughout fourteen lives, Sphere Eight decided that the time and the conditions were right to pluck this highly-evolved spiritual flower and train her for a much higher service to mankind.

We, unanimously, decided that Amanda had all the qualities necessary to become a member of the hierarchy so we 'arranged' her collection from Earth and brought her to Sphere Eight where, after a suitable period of readjustment, she spent about one hundred and sixty years of Earth time being trained and programmed for a great future. I cannot release the details of that future yet.

I, ARCHIBALD, AM THE LORD GOD. My activities are featured very prominently in the bible. Owing to the diabolical ignorance of the people in those days there was a great need for direct intervention on my part. Today, because of much improved education and knowledge, generally, I have no need to resort to the drama of biblical times.

First, I shall try to clarify the difference between me and God on Plane Seven, who most people believe created Heaven and Earth and to whom people pray. I did not create Heaven and Earth either, therefore it is reasonable to suppose that there is a Supreme Being, in a Higher Sphere than mine, who DID create the universe and everything and everyone in it. Presumably, our Creator does not wish to make Himself known.

God, Zaugel, Hildon, Gailbron and I have never had physical bodies but we have all been created by our anonymous Creator. I realize that this will be very difficult to understand and will take a lot of thinking about but the information contained in this course is intended to be a Handbook of Life, not only for the spiritual, heavenly life but for your material, earthly life as well.

Zaugel, Hildon, Gailbron and I have been closely connected and involved with the physical universe from the moment of our own creation. We have always been High Spiritual Beings and we were the four 'living creatures' described by Ezekiel in his book in the bible. I spoke to Abraham, Moses and Ezekiel, among others, as well as declaring to the crowds that Jesus Christ was my Beloved Son in whom I was well pleased. Unfortunately, this has been interpreted rather too literally as spiritual beings cannot reproduce, but crass ignorance prevailed and it was necessary to use parables, word pictures or metaphors that could be understood.

God on Plane Seven has dealt fully, in Lesson Eleven, with His duties and role in Heaven. God and I work very closely together. When Amanda volunteered to be reincarnated into her present life for a special purpose, I asked God to give her careful attention throughout her time on Earth.

God and His large staff deal with all individual prayers, the planning of kharmas and genetic evolution.

I, and my team of Gardeners in Sphere Eight, govern the whole of the heavenly universe in which *we* live and the physical universe in which *you* live.

This latter work is extremely difficult as the majority of the inhabitants of Earth have brown auras, representing the lowest types, determined to be as recalcitrant as possible. They are learning, or not learning, their lessons in life; they are atoning for their crimes committed at some period in their existence and are usually creating more crimes to be atoned for in yet more lives in the future, while others are hell-bent on the destruction of their environment and everyone in it.

Virtually every religion on Earth is claimed, by its leaders, to be the only true religion. Some of them claim that anyone not adhering to their particular creed is doomed to burn in Hell and can never achieve salvation. What they do NOT realize is that the Hell they talk about is of their own making, as the planet Earth is the one and only Hell.

All references in the Old Testament of the bible to people talking to 'God' describe encounters with me. I mention in particular Abraham, Moses and Ezekiel who are with me in Sphere Eight. The Old Testament is full of descriptions of spaceships landing and taking off with thunderous noises, earth quaking, great clouds of dust, hot ground and loud voices speaking from above. All are graphic, eye-witness accounts of spaceships, which are not new.

The voices heard were mine and those of the High Spiritual Beings who were in the ship with me. We were giving orders over our public address system. References to people sitting on the right hand of God are to those with whom I had to have long discussions. I invited them inside the ship to discuss their problems with me. Among these were Moses, Abraham and Ezekiel who were chosen by me for special purposes. They sat on my right because the spaceships of that time were controlled by the pilot sitting in the left-hand seat.

When Jesus Christ was put into the tomb we had to act quickly in order to save Him. He was in an unconscious state, having suffered terrible agony and loss of blood. Zaugel, Hildon, Gailbron and I swiftly came to the rescue in a spaceship. Our machines are hemispherical in shape and appear to shine brightly in the sky owing to radiated, spiritual power. We landed the spaceship silently, as it was very early morning. We had no wish to cause premature alarm by alerting the guards. Zaugel approached the tomb and put the guards to sleep by a very powerful thought process, then he rolled the heavy stone away by the use of a spiritual repellent beam.

At this point, Jesus Christ's mother and Mary Magdalene appeared. Zaugel sat on the stone and spoke quietly and calmly to them. In the gospel according to Matthew, Chapter 28, verses 2 and 3 it states, 'And behold there was a great earthquake for the angel of the Lord descended from Heaven and came and rolled back the stone from the door and sat upon it. His countenance was like lightning, and his raiment as white as snow.'

Mark, Chapter 16, verse 5 states, 'And entering into the sepulchre, they saw a young man, sitting on the right side, clothed in a long white garment.'

John, Chapter 20, verse 12 states, 'And seeth two angels in white sitting, the one at the head, and the other at the feet, where the body of Jesus had lain.'

When I saw that Zaugel was unexpectedly confronted by those two women, I walked from the spaceship in case he needed any help. After speaking comfortingly to the two Marys and sending them on their way, we entered the tomb. Zaugel picked up Jesus Christ and carried Him to the spaceship. We mocked up a noise during take-off in order to create an awesome effect on the people present. This is referred to in the gospels of the New Testament as an earthquake. We flew Jesus Christ to India and, during the flight, Hildon and Gailbron gave Him intensive healing.

An examination of the gospels reveals many discrepancies in the account of Jesus Christ's disappearance. This is because of the usual distortion of facts owing to messages being passed by word of mouth. Also, the events taking place were beyond the comprehension of the people.

While the writing of our scripts for this work was in progress, a programme about UFOs was televised, in which a lady gave an excellent description of me in my spaceship. She described my ship as being like a Mexican hat, which it does rather resemble. She said she could see two people in the cockpit while the ship hovered silently over her house. She described us as "beautiful people."

One was I, Archibald, the Lord God and Officer-in-Charge of Sphere Eight, the other was Zaugel. We make periodic visits to observe conditions on Earth and deliberately let people see us. We want incarnate people to realize that there are more things in Heaven and Earth than they are aware of.

My name, 'Archibald', means genuine and bold. I chose it when my three companions and I decided that we must have some means of identification. My team of Gardeners in Sphere Eight always address me as Mr Archibald. The correct form of address to the inhabitants of our particular Sphere is to prefix the name with the word 'Mister', for example, Mr Abraham, Mr Isaac, Mr Moses and so on. However, to try to simplify matters for all incarnate persons everywhere, I wish to be known as the Lord God because I AM YOUR LORD GOD.

It is understandable how confusion arose over the use of the term 'God' in the book of Genesis which was not written by Moses but by priests and scribes much later in time. The word 'God' means a superhuman being, an object of worship. Therefore, as our Creator was responsible for the Creation, the term 'God' was erroneously ascribed to Him.

This is the first, quite pardonable, error in the bible. Others will be clarified by my colleagues as they write their scripts through Amanda. It should, by now, be abundantly apparent why it was necessary to pay such special attention to Amanda Valiant's present life. Without her highly-specialized training and programming by us, which was retained in her subconscious mind at her birth in 1925, this knowledge could not have been given to your world; neither would the opportunity have arisen for the gross errors in popular belief to be corrected.

As in Jesus Christ's case, neither He nor Amanda could consciously remember for what they were on Earth. Each knew they had a purpose but memory is suppressed before reincarnation so that previous life existences and life in Heaven remain subliminal.

This is done by God and is necessary because life in Heaven is so much better than on Earth that, if people remembered it too clearly, they would not wish to remain for their allotted time span on the Earth planet. Furthermore, all atrocious suffering experienced in previous lives would be too vivid and painful to remember in present time.

In conclusion, I wish to state that there is no need for a mass panic over this new information. In order to try to clarify the apparent irregularity of three Gods in Heaven, let me propose the following analogy.

Think of our Creator as the Founder and Principal of a Giant Company, of my team of Gardeners as the Board of Directors and of me, the Lord God, as their Chairman with God of Plane Seven as the Managing Director.

In this lesson, for the first time in history, the puzzling aspects of biblical accounts have been clarified. Many of the so-called 'visions' of people were, in fact, realities. These realities were so astounding that they were mis-reported and misunderstood by witnesses. It will repay the student to study all of the available data on UFOs because many of the sightings are of the Lord God's spaceship in modern times.

Lesson 13   **Part Two**

THE INHABITED PLANETS

Intelligent beings throughout the entire universe are all in human form, varying only within relatively small ranges of size and weight. For a planet to sustain human biological forms, it must provide an environment capable of supplying the comparatively narrow range of conditions necessary to sustain life.

The size of an inhabitable planet is governed by the average mass of a human being. If, for example, a person weighs seventy kilograms on Earth, his muscular strength is capable of supporting that weight. If he were to try to live on a planet of twice the mass of the Earth, his effective weight would be one hundred and forty kilograms and he would hardly be able to stand up. Such a planet would have a diameter of only approximately sixteen thousand kilometres or ten thousand miles compared with the Earth's thirteen thousand kilometres or eight thousand miles. Lifting weights and climbing hills would become almost impossible and vehicles would need twice the horse power of an Earth vehicle to climb the same gradient with wide tracks to prevent them from sinking into the surface.

On a smaller planet than Earth, people would weigh less and would find no difficulty in moving large objects but their stability on the ground would be impaired and they might bounce when walking.

For human survival in natural conditions, there must be a plentiful and constantly self-renewing supply of oxygen within fairly close pressure limits. If the atmospheric pressure were so high that the partial pressure of the oxygen approached twice that on Earth the body would be adversely affected by oxygen toxicity. If the oxygen partial pressure were excessively low, the cells of the human body and brain would atrophy owing to hypoxia.

An inert gas equivalent to nitrogen which represents seventy-nine per cent of the Earth's atmosphere is also necessary to provide enough bulk of gas for the lungs to function correctly.

Vegetation is necessary in order to produce, by photosynthesis, oxygen to replace that converted into carbon dioxide by combustion of all kinds including the metabolic processes in animal and human bodies. Water is essential to sustain life, so there must be an unlimited supply of fresh drinking water, the result of a sea, cloud and rain cycle.

The extreme temperature range on Earth is from about minus fifty degrees Celsius to roughly fifty degrees Celsius but comfort is only possible between about nought degrees Celsius and thirty-two degrees Celsius. The temperature range on a planet is largely determined by its proximity to its own sun and the composition and density of its atmosphere.

Although there are hundreds of thousands of planets in the universe, few have the conditions just described. Some have no atmosphere and others have a dense, unbreathable atmosphere that results in such violent weather conditions that survival would be impossible. It can be seen that, since the requirements for human existence fall within such relatively narrow bands, the chances of finding a large number of inhabited planets are, statistically, reduced enormously.

Only Earth men are warlike at the present time. The inhabitants of the other planets, although they have warred in the very distant past, are now all peaceable.

Earth, the punishment planet, is the odd one out and, for the student's interest, here is a list of all the inhabited planets in the entire universe:

Yolland Allicay, Fos, Sol, Coul,
Bos, Tet, Earth, Moon.

Yolland Allicay, known as the reward planet, is in the same solar system as Fos. Sol and Coul are in a different solar system in another galaxy. Bos and Tet are in a third solar system in a further galaxy. Earth is the only human-inhabited planet in its solar system and its galaxy.

The moon is a unique case. Some of the evidence brought back to Earth by the spacemen sent to investigate it has been deliberately suppressed by governments because they found out that there were men already there!

The moon IS inhabited on the inside by about two hundred men. There is a man-made covering around the moon which is several kilometres deep in order to protect the inhabitants from meteoric bombardment. It was guided to its present position about ten thousand years ago.

The moon is a small planet which has been enlarged and built upon by people originating from Yolland Allicay. They built a spaceship and travelled to this small planet which was orbiting another planet in the region of Yolland Allicay. A protective shield, approximately seven kilometres deep, was built around the planet, fully encasing it. The casing consisted largely of titanium and took many generations of people to build. Their supplies were drawn partly from this new planet and partly from Yolland Allicay, the inhabitants of which were very highly developed in their technology and, by applying their skills in this field, discovered that there were other inhabited planets.

The moon-men are tall and very pale-faced. As they live right inside the moon, they are constantly in artificial light. Their eyes take on a pinkish hue because of their unnatural lighting conditions. Their spaceships are kept inside the moon. The moon-men are not at all hostile but can defend themselves with formidable force should they be provoked FIRST.

The script that follows was written, posthumously, by the eminent engineer Isambard Kingdom Brunel, well known on Earth in the nineteenth century. He obtained the information after studying the Akashic Record.

> I, Isambard Kingdom Brunel, am writing this through Alan Valiant. On being asked to examine the Akashic Record in order to discover exactly how the moon was put into its present orbit around the Earth, I went to the Hall of Memories and studied the Record.
>
> I discovered that, about ten thousand years ago, the moon was not circling the Earth. Then, on further inves-

tigation, I traced the moon back to when it was in another galaxy.

The moon originated in the vicinity of Yolland Allicay and was taken over by space travellers from Allicay. The moon was, then, a slightly smaller planet but it was unoccupied by any form of life. The Allicayans were able to survive after creating an atmosphere around the planet that they could breathe. This was done by a gas-generating process which produced an oxygen-rich atmosphere.

As they had a very advanced technology and had been using spaceships for thousands of years, the Allicayans knew that the planet Earth existed and decided to investigate it. They agreed to put their new-found planet in orbit around the Earth and use it as a space station, for which purpose it has been used ever since.

With material existing on the embryo moon and with enormous quantities of titanium flown in from Allicay, a shield, about seven kilometres thick, was built around the entire surface of the planet. This work was facilitated by the relatively low gravitational pull of the moon but was, nevertheless, an enormous task and took approximately two thousand years to complete.

The shield was for two purposes. The first was to protect the population from meteoric bombardment which, it was known, would occur during the journey through space to Earth. The other was so as to provide living space in the moon capable of holding an artificially-created, breathable atmosphere.

The spaceships are powered by a system yet unknown to earthmen. The same techniques of harnessing enormous power have been in use by spacemen for millions of years. Expressed very basically, there is a matrix of invisible lines of power that pervade space throughout the entire universe. By the utilization of a highly technical method, the power control apparatus in the spacecraft resolves the lines of power into a rapid succession of three-dimensional co-ordinates. After further processing, this information is fed to the leading and trailing surfaces of the craft in such a form that it produces a differential of space potential that induces thrust.

In a similar manner to the creation of lift on the wing of an aeroplane, that is by differential pressure, the spacecraft develops the equivalent of a low pressure ahead and a higher pressure aft and this propels it. All major heavenly bodies are held in their relative positions in space by gravitational forces which are invisible, but nevertheless effective, and the lines of power are coincident with and analogous with these forces.

Once freed from the gravitational effects of its parent planet, the small satellite needed virtually no power to keep it moving. The journey lasted only about two Earth years. This may seem absolutely unbelievable to Earth scientists but the fact is that the moon and the spaceships were able to travel faster than the speed of light. Contrary to popular, present-day belief, physical matter can travel faster than light and the Allicayans knew the secrets of such travel.

Using tremendous skill, they brought the moon near to the Earth and gradually eased it into orbit around the Earth. The moon's present orbit is very nearly circular and could not have occurred naturally. After having put their space base into its proper orbit, they corrected its tendency to spin because they wanted to operate from the side never seen from Earth.

These people were very far-sighted and knew that one day Earth men would reach the moon. The descendants of the original pioneer Allicayans are still occupying the moon which has been continuously manned since its first appearance in the sky above Earth.

Scientists and engineers on Earth still have a great deal to learn about space travel. However, some people on Earth are already aware of the existence of the men in the moon but, as usual, they fear them. They are not to be feared. They are highly intelligent and have no wish to harm people. They would always come off best in any attempt to harm *them,* though. They can use their mental abilities to the full and are quite capable of incapacitating Earth people by a thought process, rendering the use of weapons unnecessary.

I, Isambard Kingdom Brunel, well-known engineer of the nineteenth century, am now occupied designing spaceships for the Gardeners of the Earth. I build them from spiritual matter. The ships are very similar in appearance to those used by the moon men but theirs are physical machines built from materials similar to those found on Earth.

UFOs are with you and have been for thousands of years. If they had wished, the occupants could have taken over Earth several millennia ago. It is up to incarnate man to accept that he is not the only human creature in the Universe. He has his counterparts who look almost exactly like Earth men, scattered among the other inhabited planets. Not until this fact is accepted will man lose his morbid fear of being attacked by a superior, exterior force.

* * *

This is Alan Valiant's soulmate, Tena, writing through him about the men in the moon. I have just been to the moon in my spiritual form and have watched the inhabitants for some time. I saw men in silver uniforms, wearing space helmets, leaving a spaceship in which they had just arrived.

The ship was flown down into an enormous hole on the far side of the moon from Earth. Then, the occupants came out of the spaceship and entered a compartment in which they were pressurized to the normal pressure inside their living area. They breathe air and have created an artificial environment which includes simulated sunlight.

As I watched, the men walked into another room and boarded a kind of train. This carried them some long distance inside the moon until they came to a brightly illuminated hall. On leaving the train, they undressed and put on clean overalls, packing their space suits into boxes already provided.

Then the men, four in number, went to a room and had some food. They were talking about their recent journey in a language not known on Earth. I could understand them because I have no language difficulties as a spiritual being.

They were discussing their visit to Earth which had just been completed. Apparently, they were ordered to proceed to South America to a place in the Andes, there to meet one of their own men who had been left there to study conditions. They had brought him back and he was the fourth man.

There are about two hundred men inside the moon and they have approximately twenty-five spaceships in operation. Some were in maintenance areas deep in the bowels of the moon and others were at readiness in the great entrance hole.

There are no women or children inside the moon. The men work to a rota system and are sent from another planet to serve so many months, or perhaps years, on the moon after which they return to their own planet.

There are large laboratories and briefing and debriefing rooms in the sub-lunar environment. Engineering workshops are fully manned and are busy turning out replacement components for the spaceships.

The moon men do not intend to harm Earth people and have no weapons that I could see. They are endowed with a very, very high intelligence and are far superior to Earth men in every way. They dare not declare themselves because the Earth people would only fear them and attempt to exterminate them.

Lesson 14   Part Two
MOSES AND THE COMMANDMENTS

Introduction

The following script was taken by Madam Amanda Valiant before her passing and is here reproduced verbatim.

The student is advised to read the chapter of Exodus in the bible and compare the descriptions of the events with those described by Moses himself in this lesson.

This is Moses writing through Amanda Valiant while she is still incarnate. I wrote the book of Exodus in the bible and called it that because it deals with the exit of the children of Israel from Egypt. It is the only book in the bible that I wrote, no others were written by me.

The story of my birth and how I was put into a basket by my mother and floated away downstream, is true. Pharaoh's daughter saw the basket containing me drifting downstream and sent her maid to fetch it. Pharaoh's daughter brought me up and, in effect, adopted me for I was very well treated by her.

When I grew up, I killed an Egyptian in a fight because he was striking one of my own kind and getting the upper hand. My crime was discovered and the news of it reached Pharaoh's ears. This upset him so much that I had to leave rather hurriedly.

I eventually married and my wife and I were very happy. My main occupation was to look after the sheep of my father-in-law. One day I led them rather a long way off and, while I was resting, a spaceship arrived. The 'burning bush' story in the bible is based on an illusion. The spacecraft landed behind the bushes and well away from them. Looking at this sight from a distance, it seemed to me that the bushes were on fire, yet they were not being burnt. Curious, I went nearer to investigate. This was meant to be, of course! Naturally, I was a bit frightened but curiosity ruled the day and got the better of me. I heard my name called, so I answered.

I was told not to come near. The 'holy ground' was extremely hot from the flames that were shooting down from the amazing spectacle before me. Exodus, Chapter 3, verse 5.

The 'God' who spoke to me was Mr Archibald, the Lord God. He told me that my job was to lead the Israelites out of Egypt because they were such an oppressed people. Upon asking why I had been chosen, I was told not to argue. Mr Archibald promised me plenty of support. All references in my book to Lord God, Lord or God, refer to Mr Archibald.

In trying to evade responsibility for the arduous task which was being demanded of me, I wanted proof from Mr Archibald that He could keep His promises. The stories of my rod being changed into a serpent and my hand becoming leprous are true. This was my proof but I was still unhappy about my unexpected situation and tried to argue with the Lord God that I was not eloquent enough, nor quick-witted enough, for the task that He had set me. Mr Archibald then became rather impatient and arranged for my brother, Aaron, who was educated, to help me. Clearly, He had no intention of letting me off the hook!

It pleased me that my brother should help me in this work and we met later. Aaron and I went to Pharaoh and pleaded with him to let the Israelites go free. We went many times to argue with him and his advisors which resulted in several fights.

The accounts of the plagues sent to try the Egyptians are true, with the exception of the locust story. The plague of locusts was a natural phenomenon and nothing to do with spiritual interference. Mr Archibald, the Lord God, did *not* harden Pharaoh's heart. If Pharaoh had a heart at all, it was like a stone. He was a wicked ruler, a megalomaniac and he can be likened to certain twentieth-century dictators, to give you an idea.

The plagues finally wore down the resistance of Pharaoh and the Egyptians and we left Egypt. With Mr Archibald in His spaceship leading us, we made our way to the Red Sea which was crossed at its narrowest part. The description in the bible of 'the cloud by day and the fire by night' refers to the spaceship leading us. At night it shone brightly because of spiritual radiance; by day smoke poured from it at intervals giving the appearance of clouds.

The division of the Red Sea was achieved by atomic power. We Gardeners can control matter at an atomic level, therefore nothing is impossible to Mr Archibald, the Lord God or to our Creator whose total power must not be underestimated. An atomic explosion occurred, causing neither radiation nor fall-out and it was powerful enough to raise the sea bed, thus dividing the water. The ground was not dry but a muddy mess.

Some of the Egyptians followed us but were frightened by the explosion and others stayed on the bank or shore. Those who did follow us were caught in the natural subsidence of the exposed sea bed and were drowned. The people whom I delivered thought that I was a God and knelt down and worshipped me. They thought I, Moses, had done all these things and that I was a man of war. That was not true.

My sister and I met again at this time and there was a tearful reunion. We were parted when I was very young and I was overwhelmed and overjoyed to see her again. She was a few years older than I was and she told me what had happened to me after my mother put me in the basket. My mother possessed psychic powers and instinctively knew that I *had* to be saved as I was rather 'special'. I told my sister that I thought she was clever to offer to find a nurse for me and then to run and fetch my mother. Her prompt and clever action saved my life.

After the crossing of the Red Sea, Mr Archibald

landed His spaceship on Mount Sinai. I went up to meet Him and He handed me some granite slabs with a code of behaviour written on them for the people to follow. When I came down from the mountain, I found the people worshipping false gods and images which made me very, very angry as Aaron and I had worked extremely hard to get them away from their Egyptian suppressors. In my anger, I smashed the stones. Aaron found it difficult to keep the people under control while I was in conference with Mr Archibald at the top of Mount Sinai and had to let them do more or less as they liked for the sake of peace.

I ordered all the people who were willing to come with me to do so, and those who were not willing set upon those who were, resulting in yet another fight. I did not order anybody to be killed, that is a fabrication.

A tabernacle is a kind of portable church and mine was a tent set aside for the purpose. Mr Archibald came again to Mount Sinai in His spaceship and we discussed plans for making new tablets of stone. Working together, we engraved the same set of rules on them as before but it took a long time. When we had completed the work, I came down from Mount Sinai a happy and pleased individual, having spent so much time in the company of a Very High Spiritual Being, which always uplifts people.

The Lord God, in His spaceship, remained with us for a short while after we had founded a church for the people to give thanks for what had been done for them. This accounts for the 'cloud' over the tabernacle. The 'glory of the Lord' filling the tabernacle was the glowing reflection of the spaceship and the 'fire by night' was the flames from the ship.

I shall now go into detail about the Ten Commandments which I brought down from Mount Sinai and which Mr Archibald, the Lord God, *not* God, gave to me. Exodus, Chapter 20 deals with this.

Formal education was unheard of, except for those of very good families and high birth, so ignorance abounded and Aaron and I had our work cut out to handle the savage people. In order to make them give up their idol worshipping, I told them they must not worship any other god but the one in Heaven, meaning the one from the sky who had brought them out of their bondage, hence the law, 'Thou shalt have no other gods before me.' Exodus, Chapter 20, verse 3.

The second commandment is self-explanatory. I was telling them to stop making idols. Verse 4.

The reference to taking God's name in vain meant that I was trying to explain that they should not blaspheme, swear at God or use His name in emptiness and without a feeling of reverence. Verse 7.

'Remember the Sabbath day, to keep it holy.' We wanted one day each week set aside for reflection on what had been done for the people. They were to work during the other six days. By now, we had worked out a more accurate method of recording time.

'Honour thy father and thy mother,' was our way of saying, 'Be good to your parents who have spent their lives bringing up families and who should be shown some consideration in their old age.' Verse 12.

'Thou shalt not kill!' Verse 13, was intended by the Lord God to mean, 'You must not murder each other' and should not be interpreted as meaning that animals must not be killed for food.

The next two commandments are self-explanatory and I need not dwell on them. Verses 14 and 15.

'Thou shalt not bear false witness against thy neighbour.' In this case, I was telling them not to tell falsehoods about others with a view to causing them harm. Verse 16.

'Thou shalt not covet thy neighbour's house, thou shalt not covet thy neighbour's wife, nor his manservant, nor his maidservant, nor his ox, nor his ass, nor anything that is thy neighbour's.' Here, I was instructing them not to be jealous or envious of other people's property because everyone had the same chance to get what they wanted if they worked hard enough for it.

I wish to suggest here and now some rules more applicable to modern living:

1. Show consideration and kindness for the elderly and infirm because many of them have devoted their lives to giving their children every opportunity.
2. Do not kill people, except in self-defence or in defending one's family and property. It is not a crime to kill animals for food, humanely. Pests like rats, locusts, flies and mosquitoes are rightly exterminated as they cause damage and disease.
3. In these days of modern living we cannot enforce 'No adultery'. Adultery is the act of intercourse with a person other than the legal husband or wife. I want to stress that marriage is desirable because it is a contract between two people who should know whether or not they are sufficiently suited to one another to spend the rest of their lives together without wanting anyone else. Longer courtships and more control over the emotions are necessary to achieve this. Broken homes mean untold misery and hardship and prevention is better than cure.
4. Do not steal.
5. Do not lie. Lies and deceit cause mistrust and distress. If everyone were open and above board, communication would be much easier and more pleasant.
6. Jealousy, envy, hatred, bitterness and despair are negative emotions to be avoided. Have an earnest desire to work and save for the things required, instead of envying other people.
7. Obtain the highest standard of integrity possible by becoming honest, pure-minded, courteous and kind.
8. Unselfishness is desirable. A general improvement in

one's own spiritual level will result from turning one's attention to others. One needs to accept responsibility for one's own actions instead of blaming everything and everyone else. Vandals seem to think society should carry them so they take what they think is revenge and give nothing in return.

9. Strive to attain beauty in all things. For example: music, art, painting, sculpture, books, magazines, films, television and radio. Fight against the low standards prevailing today and bring back the qualities of beauty and goodness in everything, stressing the finer aspects of man's character.

10. Keep a healthy and active mind all through life, even in retirement. Learning is a continuing process that transcends 'death'.

The following script was taken by Madam Amanda Valiant before her passing and is here reproduced verbatim.

This is Ezekiel writing through Amanda Valiant while she is still incarnate. My book in the bible is in the wrong place and should be in the New Testament as I wrote some of it in AD 100. I made frequent references, in my writings at that time, to Jesus Christ but these have been altered by priests and scribes to read 'Lord God'. I think that the reason for these alterations was probably because any reference to Jesus Christ materializing His spiritual body so long after His crucifixion and so-called 'death' was a forbidden subject and I suspect that a certain amount of guilt was felt at the way He had been treated.

In chapter one of my book, I described the events listed there *as they actually happened.* They were not 'visions' given to me in a dream, neither were they figments of my imagination. I consider that I did a remarkable job of reporting, considering the limitations of our vocabulary at that time. It may be compared with attempting to describe interplanetary warfare in Elizabethan English!

The priests and elders of the AD 268 convocation did a very great deal of harm to the scriptures as you know them today. The scribes of our time were the present-day equivalent of newspaper reporters who are well known for their sensationalism and unreliability. The unscrupulous scribes, in collaboration with priests and high officials of the church, decided that which should be written and that which should be omitted, therefore what emerged from their writings was a very garbled version of the truth.

I was standing by the river Chebar one day when I saw, as I know now, a spaceship arrive with four people on board. They were, as I learned later, Mr Archibald, the Lord God and my present colleagues in Sphere Eight; Zaugel, Hildon and Gailbron. My description that each one had 'four faces' referred to their helmets, the front aperture of which showed their own face while on the other three sides were emblems of a lion, an ox and an eagle. A present-day comparison is the national emblem worn by men from Earth when they are travelling in space. Each astronaut wears on his suit the emblem of the flag of his country. Each of the men had the means to propel himself through the air independently which I described as their wings. On their feet were special boots which, to me, resembled calves' feet.

I was a very good psychic when I was incarnate and I hope that you have noticed, by this time in our scripts, that all the Gardeners of the Earth who have had lives on Earth possessed remarkable psychic vision. The people whom I described in chapter one of my book were materialized High Spiritual Beings and the spacecraft and all the equipment that they were using had been manufactured in the spiritual universe. Then the Lord God spoke to me. I realized that I was being chosen to do something special and, as all this was so awesome to me, I promptly fell on my face with fear. This was to be the greatest test and task of my life.

Mr Archibald had arrived with my orders to enter Israel to try to educate the ignorant and rebellious masses living there. He gave me refreshment and spread before me my instructions, written on a kind of rice paper. I was asked to memorize the contents of the paper and then eat it. This sounds rather 'cloak and daggerish' but we lived in that kind of world.

I felt very nervous about all this and, like Moses, considered that I was not competent to carry out such a tough assignment. It took me about a week to recover from the shock of that which I had seen and heard and, above all, the heavy responsibility of the task that I had been given. I wandered into what is now known as Tel Aviv and stayed there in a daze, pondering. How was I to start this momentous task? Whom could I ask, or trust, to help me? What kind of reception would I get from the savage people?

When I refer, in the bible, to the 'hand of the Lord' being upon me, I am referring to my intuition, hunches, premonitions or general psychic awareness, call it what you will. I had a strong urge to go to a quiet place and, upon my arrival, Mr Archibald, the Lord God, appeared to me again. He knew that I was troubled over the assignment and He came to offer help and encouragement. He told me that He would speak to the Israelites, through me, using me as His instrument. This is a common spiritual phenomenon and is practised by some mediums today. My reference to this can be found in Ezekiel, Chapter 3, verses 22-27.

Mr Archibald, the Lord God, took me into His spaceship and flew me over Jerusalem to show me all the dreadful things that went on there. Ezekiel, Chapter 8, refers.

The Israelites were confirmed idol worshippers and had to be threatened severely with all sorts of dreadful punishments if they did not forsake their evil ways. These threats were not carried out unless it became obvious that there was no other way of bringing them to order and obedience.

Having been suitably encouraged and cheered by the Lord God, I entered Jerusalem to begin my work. Mr Archibald joined me and, although I could see Him, He was not visible to the masses. Mr Archibald spoke to the people by taking over my vocal cords. Using this method of communication we spent some considerable time lecturing the inhabitants about their disgraceful behaviour. The Lord God firmly laid down the law with them and threatened dire punishments if they did not conform to His wishes.

In Ezekiel, Chapter 36, verse 23 to the end of that chapter, the tone of the statements alters because, at this point, Jesus Christ materialized to me and stayed with me for a number of days. He understood my predicament and, having been in a somewhat similar position Himself when He was incarnate, He came to help and succour me.

From verse twenty-three to the conclusion of that chapter, is a report of a conversation between Jesus Christ and me. We were discussing, in the quaint tongue of the time, the possibilities of what life *could* be like for the Israelites if they behaved themselves and conformed to the Lord God's wishes. Jesus Christ was giving me an idea of what to say to these people and references to Lord God or God in that part of the chapter mean Jesus Christ. I am, now, a Gardener of the Earth and a kinsman of Jesus Christ.

There are two ways in which spiritual beings can materialize so that they are visible on Earth. One is to materialize in the form of the last physical body that the person had on Earth and the other is to materialize the spiritual body but this can only be done by a High Spiritual Being. This has a very different appearance from that of a materialized physical body and accounts for the references to faces looking like brass or being illuminated in some way.

The man described in Ezekiel, chapter 40, verse 3 was Jesus Christ in His spiritual form and I quote, 'And he brought me thither, and behold, there was a man, whose appearance was like the appearance of brass, with a line of flax in his hand, and a measuring reed; and he stood in the gate.' The measurements that were being taken were for the redesigning of the city of Jerusalem and Jesus Christ and I were the chief designers. Mr Archibald suggested that a new Jerusalem be built and He helped us with the design work and approved it when it was finished.

The first twelve chapters in my book are authentic and have been quite well written and preserved from my original writings. The remainder of my book has been altered, embellished, mistranslated and falsified by the priests, elders and scribes of the AD 268 convocation.

Anything that was not understood by them was either omitted or altered to suit *their* purposes. Information about reincarnation and materializations of the so-called dead was suppressed because these subjects were completely and absolutely misunderstood. They did not want people to know that it was Jesus Christ who appeared to me, even though I stated this in my writings.

I am very pleased to have had this opportunity of straightening the record through the knowledge and understanding of our two instruments on earth namely, Amanda and Alan Valiant without whom it would not have been possible.

Lesson 15   **Part Two**

WHY RELIGIONS, AND INDIVIDUAL PERSONALITY

Why Religions?

From time immemorial man has had a compelling desire to worship but first let us define the word 'worship'. The dictionary describes it as 'adoration paid, as to a god, profound admiration, act of revering, to idolize.' What makes man admire, revere or idolize anyone? Is it genuine admiration or could it be fear?

Everyone has their own particular way of reacting when in a situation of fear. The courageous may merely flick an eyelid, the not-so-brave may break into a sweat and look for escape; while the coward, self-confessed or not, may utter a shriek and take to his heels.

The student may ask what all this has to do with religion. Fear and suppression have been the predominant means of controlling the religious throughout the world for centuries. All too often, we have heard the clergy implore us to, "Pray, for you are miserable sinners." A very large proportion of their congregations may not be miserable and, as for being sinners, we all do or say something at some time in our lives which, later, we regret. Some realize the errors they have made and will make every endeavour to compensate suitably those against whom they have sinned which is very commendable, especially if the action has been motivated without any outside influence.

Fear and domination are still prevalent in present-day religions and the amazing fact seems to be that devotees are willing to accept this situation. They will cheerfully part with a percentage of their income to support their church and will agree that any children born will be brought up in that particular faith, regardless of the fact that the newly-born has a mind, a will and the right to make its own choice. These two examples amount to oppression, so why do they tolerate it? The answer will almost certainly contain a suggestion of profound admiration for the officiating cleric. The extremist will openly display adoration amounting to idolatry of the religious hierarchy or their representatives. This appears to me to be breaking the first commandment, 'Thou shalt have no other gods before me.'

Many people refrain from attending church because the orthodox, established religions do not appear to offer what they are seeking, hence the reason for the startling number of unorthodox societies and sects that have appeared during recent decades. The followers of these religions are all seeking something. The paths are many and varied but they all stop short of the promised spiritual haven.

It has been my experience in life to find that the happiest and most understanding of persons have been those who were not religiously inclined. These fortunate people have more to offer to their fellow men, merely by the example they set in the lives that they lead, than those who are steeped in religion and who hide behind closed doors and drawn curtains quietly suffering under its yoke. For suffer some of them do, as in the case of an acquaintance of mine who was thrown out of his religious sect because he dared to attend a meeting of another denomination. It was decreed by the officials of this extreme society that "he broke bread with unbelievers!"

It is a regrettable fact that both religion and politics are the downfall of Earth. Wherever a coup has occurred in the world, the reason has stemmed from either a religious or a political source and, in some instances, both have been instrumental. As religions seem to cause so much dissention among individuals, even nations, why must we have them?

Religions, in general, make no attempt to clarify the mysteries for their congregations but merely leave people in a state of fear and uncertainty as to what to expect when they depart this life. From the pulpit every Sunday, with monotonous regularity, much is said about 'everlasting life' and 'the life hereafter' but when someone who knows tries to explain what this REALLY means, down come the shutters of disbelief. Ridicule and accusations of 'devil's work' follow, flowing from the lips of 'God's chosen ones' and falling, I regret to say, all too often on ears only too ready to listen. The inability of the subdued victims of religion to discern fact from fiction is a pathetic situation.

Most churches have bible study groups who hold weekly meetings to try to understand the bible. It is a case of the blind leading the blind, for the bible is not the word of God. He did not write it, nor any part of it and, as long as anyone totally accepts that it is His word, then the mistakes contained in this world-wide volume will never be clarified.

The bible is a collection of books of the time, that is what the word 'bible' means. I could take a selection of books and arrange for them to be printed and bound into one volume. Having done this, I could then present it to the uninitiated and say, "Look! Here is the bible!" How would they know any differently?

The willingness of the masses to follow a regime already set up for them relieves them of the responsibility of thinking for themselves. This is rather sad because God has given everyone the ability to discern. Has any man the right to claim that he has 'holy' qualities merely because he is a priest? Yet, many believe that, if everything is left to the Church, their salvation will be assured, no matter how they behave.

It will take many centuries for a major change to occur such as the substitution of the Truth as herein contained for religion because the self-perpetuation of the religious hierarchy in their own interests will make them stand firm, whereas, with some deep thought and sensible application, they could be of tremendous help and influence in bringing about this most necessary transformation in the philosophy of life.

For many, the church plays a leading part in their social lives which, without it, might be otherwise non-existent. The social activities of churches are often very good indeed and are their saving grace. These events need not disappear altogether, for they do much good. Here again, a little sensible application is required.

Centuries ago, before legitimate forms of government were introduced, the Church ruled. It was felt by the leading officials of the day that there was a need for the people to have something or someone upon which or upon whom to depend, to lead them in times of adversity and to whom they could cling when in personal trouble. As the priests had a distinct advantage over the masses and education and knowledge of a primitive kind of medicine were virtually limited to them, it was considered expedient that the religious order should take over the role of government.

It was essential that the priests build an image around themselves and their work in order to gain confidence and admiration from their illiterate flocks. What better ruse to employ than to class themselves as 'holy men'? The introduction of various religious rites, rituals and symbolism followed, together with the all-too-familiar fear and suppression practised to this day.

In modern times there are political governments and, although religion and politics have walked hand-in-hand for centuries, there is no need for the two to continue together.

I have received scripts from some of the great religious leaders of the past and they said that they had to revise their thoughts on the spiritual existence after returning to Heaven. They sum up the principles of existence like this:

'You are all spiritual beings, residing temporarily in physical bodies for the purpose of atonement. You are immortal and can *never* cease to exist. Every act that you perform and every word you utter are recorded in the Akashic Record. You *all* have to be confronted by your past on ascending from the physical world and you *all* have to make retribution for any crimes that you may have committed. On the other hand, you will *all* receive rewards commensurate with your value as spiritual beings. This value will depend on how much good you succeeded in achieving or tried to achieve during your life on earth.'

It is an indication of the complete failure of established religions that the members of some of them continue to murder their fellow human beings merely because their religion has a different name. To say that one is fighting a religious war in the name of God, for example the Crusades, is to abuse the very nature of God and to defile the great love that He has for mankind. These religions preach brotherly love and then drag out their guns and start to maim, destroy and massacre. Not one of the participants in such barbarism and unbelievable atrocities against their fellow men will ever benefit by their actions. On arriving in Heaven, they are shown their acts of murder and destruction, recorded in the Akashic Record, and they are very quickly reincarnated in order to learn the right way to treat their fellow beings on Earth.

Individual Personality

There is much speculation among religious people in particular as to whether animals 'have souls'. They seem unable to perceive that all creatures are controlled by mind. The horse makes decisions to jump or not to jump, the butterfly decides to alight on a flower or to depart from it, the fishes in the sea are making decisions with their minds and not their brains because the brain is not the organ of thought.

All living creatures in biological forms, from the uni-cellular amoeba to the primates, are spiritual beings. No creature can live without being endowed with SPIRIT. The latter exists always and transfers at intervals of Earth time from one animal or human body to another.

Insects, birds, fish, reptiles and animals are all conscious and aware. They *experience*! They are *sentient*! All are incarnated into a body that has its own characteristics for its special form of life. The spiritual being's mind controls the species and receives sensory information from the particular aspects of the creature's bodily functions. For example, the bat utilizes sensory systems unique to flying creatures.

You must, surely, be aware that every species is perfectly adapted to its environment. This is not the result of 'evolution' but is the result of our Creator's design. Nothing, and no creature elsewhere or on Earth exists as the result of an accident. Nature is in balance, otherwise, one species would destroy another until none remained. Only man is capable of wiping out whole species through greed and wanton destruction. This is man's free will running away with him.

It may seem difficult for the reader to accept this but every living creature has its own personality. You would not think that a colony of ants could contain individual minds, but it is so. They are pre-programmed to behave according to basic, natural laws and this they do.

These individual personalities advance from a lower order of existence to a higher one and progress ever upward until they may be reincarnated as humans. Virtually all humans have existed in animal forms of various species. A human may have been a spider, fish, reptile, cow, dog or any biological species at some time in his or her past.

Owing to the fact that no experience is ever lost or wasted, your subconscious mind retains those experiences but, generally, they remain subliminal. Your first life incarnate may have been, for example, as a shellfish millions of Earth years ago, since when, you will have graduated to higher forms of life, culminating in human form.

After attaining human form, you are then given several lives in various bodies, male or female and of any race. Having sampled a few lives in human form, you are then responsible for your own future, depending on your behaviour. It is readily observable that no two dogs behave in exactly similar ways. Some are timid, others are aggressive; some are very alert and active, others are sluggish and apathetic.

Of course, as with children, the guardians of the animals can influence their behaviour. An animal that is suppressed cannot express its own character to the full any more than a child can.

Zoo keepers are well-placed to observe the different personalities of their animals. Even fish display unique, personal traits. These facts should go some way towards dispelling the false belief that animals 'have no souls'. They *are* souls, as you are!

Wilful cruelty to animals is a crime against Spiritual Law. Remember, the dog that you beat may have been a relative of yours in a previous incarnation. You must show respect for all forms of life because our Creator, in His infinite wisdom, made them all.

It may come as a shock to many people to learn that they may have existed in the form of an animal species but it is absolutely true. I know a man who, in the past, in addition to many human incarnations, had been a bird, a squirrel monkey and a fish in the sea. I know that I, too, have lived in the animal world.

You are not of today. You have existed for an immense amount of Earth time. You do *not* live one life only but numerous lives. Eternal life does not have to be earned by belief in any religious teaching; it is automatic and unavoidable. You *do* survive death! You *will* survive death!

Between incarnations, you exist in Heaven, in the world of spirit which is no less real than your physical one. The differences have already been explained in an earlier lesson but you should, by now, have learned not to fear death as it is only a return to your place of origin.

There follows your guide to Eternity. If you live your life with the stated facts always in mind, you will not go very far wrong.

YOUR GUIDE TO ETERNITY

1. You have lived before this life.
2. The majority of people will live again in new physical bodies.
3. The conditions of this world today, which you have helped to create, could be your inheritance many generations from now.
4. No sin or trespass is ever forgiven by God. *You* have to atone for *your* transgressions.
5. You reap as you sow.
6. *You* are responsible for *your* salvation.
7. Your behaviour while on earth is vital. It determines your spiritual future.

Lesson 16   **Part Two**

THE NEW BEGINNING

In this Course lies the key to a happier civilization for all who dwell on Earth. Those who take the key and open the door to what some people term 'the unknown' will experience immense spiritual uplift and gain the ability to cope with everyday problems and life in general.

It is outstandingly noticeable to Alan and to me that those who are unable to handle basic situations of life are low spiritual beings of Plane One. Their behaviour patterns typify their low spirituality. Therefore, it is essential that, if we are going to improve our lot in this world, we must learn how to climb the spiritual ladder. The higher up the spiritual scale one is, the better are the chances that this world will return to peaceful sanity.

A person who has reached the spiritual height of Plane Four while incarnate is less likely to commit a crime but an incarnate person who is only of Plane One spiritual height may commit a crime and then expect society to reward him for it. This is a hypothetical example, of course, because not all Plane One persons are necessarily evil.

If one if filled with the usual negative emotions of jealousy, hatred, greed, lust, envy, gluttony, chronic anger and bitterness, then this type of person either cannot or will not handle his immediate problems but will expect others to sort him out and practically live his life for him.

On the other hand, people of Plane Three and upwards spiritual height will prefer to work out their own troubles and try to avoid calling upon others to help them. They take the time and trouble to reason things out and to think more deeply than most.

Plane Two spiritual height persons are between the two levels of understanding. They behave and think rather better than Plane One people but have not yet cultivated the complete self-help and independence of a Plane Three person.

Unfortunately, this world has a predominance of Plane One types in it and this is why there is so much strife. These people are easily led, gregarious and sheep-like, because it is easier for them to accept the thinking of someone else than to think for themselves.

The advice given by the High Spiritual Beings in this Course should be given very careful consideration because they have had the ultimate in experience of existence; not just one life but many lives. They have given you invaluable help and knowledge. It may not be easy to follow their advice, depending on your circumstances and environment, but it is not impossible, either.

I realize that the information contained in my Course may upset quite a number of people because it runs counter to their religious creeds but, eventually, upon their return to Heaven, they will discover that it *is* the truth. Those who scoff at my high position in Heaven will have to face the reality of this fact when *they* return. Fate has a rather peculiar way of repercussing. I should like to say, here, that Jesus Christ, when He was incarnate, was called a deceiver by just such unenlightened people.

To put Jesus Christ on Earth to try to hammer into the multitudes how important it was to behave with simple propriety was as contrasting as putting a beautiful diamond tiara into a gravel pit. However, the heavenly hierarchy tried, through Him, to improve conditions.

One of the biggest faults of mankind is the lack of correct communication. Stop! Think! Listen to what is being said. How many of us half listen and do not think and reason things out sensibly when someone is trying to hold a conversation with us? Because of inattention in communication, misunderstandings occur.

Garbled and twisted conversations flare up into arguments amongst people and even war between countries. Communication is a vital art, whether it is between you and your next door neighbour or with nations or with the occupants of Heaven.

Recognizing that one has faults is another sensitive point and correcting them is a moral challenge but one which is as vital as improving communication if we are to achieve a society that is bearable in which to live.

The text above was written by Madam Amanda while incarnate.

The following text was written posthumously by Madam Amanda through Alan Valiant.

In order for peace to prevail upon the beautiful Earth given to us by our illustrious Creator, a tremendous reversal of attitudes must occur. The scepticism of scientists when confronted by anything that they cannot explain in physical terms *must* be replaced by an open-minded approach. They must admit that there is much that they do not know.

The bigotry and in-fighting between adherents of different religions and even between members of the same religion must give way to toleration but, best of all, those people should abandon their dogmatic beliefs and their utter dependence upon other beings such as Jesus Christ to save them because He cannot! They must realize that they hold their spiritual future in their own hands.

The forces of law and order must cleanse themselves of internal corruption and abide by high ethical standards while undertaking their difficult and often dangerous tasks of combating terrorism and crime.

The fight against drug abuse must be stepped up and very severe penalties must be imposed on anyone found guilty of purveying the evil weeds and addictive chemical drugs.

Similarly, the penalties for child abuse, sexual, physical or psychological, must be severe. The problem, today, is that judges are far too lenient. Some are even corrupt. Yes, from my present position in Heaven, I can see how they think and behave.

The legal professions are also tainted with corruption. There are many ethical and deeply concerned lawyers but there is a minority of crooked lawyers who put financial gain before justice, so, the criminal goes free.

Scientists and manufacturers must collaborate to prevent a catastrophic deterioration of the planet's resources. Air and sea pollution have reached very dangerous levels. Food is poisoned by insecticide sprays. The indigenous wildlife is dying out because of some farmers' greed for financial gain above every other consideration. Battery hen farms represent a great cruelty, bearing in mind the information in Lesson Fifteen.

Animals must be given rights and not be abused, tortured or killed for the satisfaction of men or women's vanity. Animal furs, crocodile skins, elephant tusks and rhinoceros horns, for example, should not be exploited. As long as there is a demand, the owners of such businesses will flourish. Modern materials are perfectly capable of being used as substitutes for the animal products just mentioned.

Terrorists *should* be executed. They represent a cancer in the side of society and are the dregs of humanity. If they used their intelligence, they could achieve virtually any aim without resorting to atrocities. Society is far too soft on murderers. They can be dispensed with, returned to Heaven, where they will be shown the error of their ways and given another chance. To keep them at great public expense, only to release them from prison to continue their evil work is folly in the greatest degree.

I shall finish this text by saying that the most important factor in a spiritual rehabilitation is the acceptance by the individual of personal responsibility. Next, a swing away from materialism and a desire to contribute to society and not to take everything possible for nothing, are absolutely essential if there is to be an improvement in living conditions on Earth.

CONCLUSION

Having had no previous experience of writing, when I was commissioned by the Gardeners of the Earth to write the truth about existence, I wondered how and where to begin. In short, I did not have the slightest idea of what to say, although I had extensive knowledge of the subject.

My Guide, seeing my dilemma, must have put the thought into my mind to ask for assistance from the great Bard of Avon, William Shakespeare. Someone prompted me, I am sure, because I suddenly found myself asking my Guide if he would fetch William Shakespeare for me.

My Guide obliged, brought along the great man and introduced us. He was dressed in his Elizabethan attire and looked very elegant. On his head was a black, velvet hat with a wide brim and a beautiful ostrich plume. Next, there was a green velvet jacket exquisitely embroidered, knickerbockers, white stockings and black shoes adorned with silver buckles.

I apologized to William for not having followed his works very closely and explained that I found the Elizabethan language more than I could cope with! To my surprise, he laughed heartily and agreed with me that it was rather difficult to understand. He said that few people, in his day, really understood their language and that, as a leading author and playwright, he felt justified in improving and embellishing it.

William graciously and enthusiastically accepted my invitation to help me write about the knowledge that I had been given and here began a most treasured friendship. As I worked with him, I learned that he is a very remarkable character, full of ready wit and joking fun, yet he can be very serious. William is a man with a deep understanding of the vicissitudes of life and, because he is a High Spiritual Being residing on Plane Six in Heaven, his emotions cover a large range. He can be merry, sad, moved to tears or banter with us in good-natured fun.

William Shakespeare is most adamant about the fact that he, and no other person, wrote his works. Whenever the name of Francis Bacon is mentioned, his little goatee beard bristles with annoyance!

Fortunate enough to have been given a good education, William made excellent use of it. He was only fifty-two when he died but those years were crammed with the fruits of his labours. William nicknamed Alan 'grammar school boy' right from the start of our association because Alan was also educated at a high-class grammar school.

The following sonnet was written by William through Alan who challenged him about the number of lines in each verse. William's good-natured chiding shone through and he said, "A sonnet will have as many lines as I say it will, grammar school boy!"

In all fairness to faithful, stoic William, I shall allow him to have the last word. After all, he has edited the entire work and, without his loyal help, I could not have done this job. Many tears have been shed, several bouts of illness endured and much pain borne. The comfort, patient gentleness and succour that have been shown to me, throughout, by my spiritual friends have been an unforgettable experience, shaping my character for the even greater task that lies ahead of me.

AMANDA VALIANT.

SONNET
by
WILLIAM SHAKESPEARE

At the beginning of time did spirit appear
Identities were assumed
Spiritual men and women took physical bodies to learn
About the universe that had always been here.

By harming others, some found it easier to survive
Here began the downfall of man.
On their return to Heaven
They found they were still alive.

Being confronted by their crimes
The law of kharma then applied
More bodies for each transgressor
To live again, so many times.

Remembering their spiritual source
Then forgetting, materialism predominated.
Property above morals and greed before generosity
A dozen lifetimes were their course.

Look at people in middle age or older!
Know you anyone who has suffered naught?
I doubt it. You and they are here to pay
For crimes committed when your hearts were colder.

Kharma complete, Heaven is your rest
For all time in a beautiful place
Full of lovely, Spiritual Beings.
Only here can you give of your best.

Heaven at its worst is no better than Earth
Lower Astral beings know this to their cost
Some strive to learn, others shirk

Alas, of these latter, there is no dearth.

So, strive to do your best
Bring light into the darkness of others
Conduct yourself as you know you should.
In Heaven, you will find new zest.

THE END